Given to :Sall

(·· ·· 107)

SVNDAY 14th JVNE 2009

Simon perlove.

A WORLD OF DIFFERENCE

Southern England
Edited by Genya Beeby & Justine Horne

 Young**Writers**

First published in Great Britain in 2008 by:
Young Writers
Remus House
Coltsfoot Drive
Peterborough
PE2 9JX
Telephone: 01733 890066
Website: www.youngwriters.co.uk

SB ISBN 978-1 84431 788 2

Foreword

Young Writers' Big Green Poetry Machine is a showcase for our nation's most brilliant young poets to share their thoughts, hopes and fears for the planet they call home.

Young Writers was established in 1991 to nurture creativity in our children and young adults, to give them an interest in poetry and an outlet to express themselves. Seeing their work in print will encourage them to keep writing as they grow, and become our poets of tomorrow.

Selecting the poems has been challenging and immensely rewarding. The effort and imagination invested by these young writers makes their poems a pleasure to enjoy reading time and time again.

Contents

Samuel Hennem (11)	37
Sarina Gurung (12)	37
Stan Rhys Brown (12)	38
Serené Adams (12)	38
Chloë Aldcroft (12)	38
Amelia Colegate (12)	39

Cove School, Farnborough

Darryl Packman (12)	39
Charlie Bluck (12)	39
Melleah Gunn (12)	40
Jade Haley (13)	40
Bradley Porter (13)	41
Holly McLeod (13)	41
Jessica Flynn (13)	41
Catherine Hunter (13)	42

Hanham High School, Bristol

Kayleigh Adams (12)	42
Oliver Adams (11)	42
Samantha Callaghan (11)	43
Adam Hulbert (12)	43
Chris Carr (12)	43
Ryan Bennett (11)	44
Kieran Coles (11)	44
Chloe Harris (11)	45
Ross Liddington (12)	45
Megan Rossiter (12)	46
Kayleigh Rimell (12)	46
Adam Hills (11)	47
Matthew Sully (11)	47
Jack Hussey (12)	48
Rhian Stowell (12)	48
Jessica Purnell (12)	48
Josh Owen (12)	49
Megan Rouch (12)	49
Adam Jukes (11)	49
Georgie Taylor (12)	50
Emma Bindon (11)	50
Courtney Eickhoff (12)	51
Charlotte Godwin (12)	51

Danielle Davey (12)	52
Kieran Hynam (12)	52
Bradley Paisey (12)	52
Mitchell Norman (11)	53
Harry Paice (12)	53
Kira Gyde (12)	53
Anna Glover (12)	54
Jake Bayly (12)	54
Ellie Haskins (12)	55
Daniel Kendall (11)	55
Katrina Zalokoski (12)	56
Ed Ansell (12)	56
Ben Wallace (12)	57
Nathan Gay (12)	57
Jamie Horgan (11)	58
Lauren Henderson (12)	58
William Arthur King (12)	59
Samantha Bryant (11)	59
Daniel Short (12)	59
Liam Robson (12)	60
Callum O'Connell (13)	60
Hannah Jefferies & Ashley Keefe (13)	61
Luke Dunning (12)	61
Fred Moore (12)	62

Ixworth Middle School, Bury St Edmunds

Rebecca Callow (11)	62
Yasmin Bridges (11)	63
Kieran Blakey (12)	63
Natasha McCarthy (11)	64
Alastair Reith (11)	64
Hannah Wright (12)	65
Anna Reeves (10)	65
Emma Victoria Simpson (12)	66
Rachel Herod (11)	66
Sophie Rochford (11)	67
Alice Neal (12)	67
Alexander Cattanach (12)	68
Emily Findlay (12) & Rosie Hopkins (11)	68
Connor Jones (12)	68
Joshua Flack (11)	69

Megan Jones (11)   69
Ellie Brookes (12)   70

Lakeside, Chandlers Ford
Billy Ashford-Webb (12)   70
Jamie Burgess (14)   71
Nathan Moroncini (12)   71

Mangotsfield School, Bristol
Josh Harrison (14)   72
Luke Bessell (14)   73
Dan Upton   74
Katie Smart (13)   74
Charlotte Wotton (13)   75
Beth Seaford (14)   75
Jack Withey (14)   76
Josh Martin (14)   77
Fleur Sherborne (14)   78
Matthew Vicker (14)   79
Jeron Taylor (14)   80
Emily Rose (14)   81
Abby Instone (14)   82
Izzy Walkley (13)   83
Samantha Douglas (13)   84
Rebecca Brain (14)   84

Marlwood School, Bristol
Katherine Gardner (11)   85
Emily Priday (11)   85
Alex Luke (11)   86
Matthew Holliday (11)   86
Katie Moore (11)   87

Newlands Girls' School, Maidenhead
Emma Johnson (17)   87
Zoë Jacobs (16)   88
Hannah Cheeseman (12)   88

The Castle School, Bristol

Amy Stockford (12)	89
James Gay (12)	89
Georgia Honey (12)	90
Elisabeth Caise (12)	90
Freya Shearman (12)	91
Brenna Harcom (12)	91
James Baxter (12)	92
Matthew Whiles (11)	92
Charlie Tilleard & Hannah Gibbens (13)	93
Emily Savery (11)	93
Natasha Skinner (12)	94
Sophie Vaughan-Williams (12)	95
Izzie Boulton (13)	95
Amy Follows (11)	96
Alice Rose Cottle (13)	96
Matt Roberts (12)	97
Hannah Coghlan (13)	97
Stuart James (13)	98
Ella-May Cleaver (12)	98
Ella King (13)	98
Sam Mindenhall (12)	99
Jemma Campbell (12)	99
Katie Walker (13)	100
Luke Panting (12)	100
Iris McNeill (13)	101
Jody Wheeler	101
Hannah Moore (13)	102
Yasmin Thatcher & Natasha Taylor (13)	102
Christopher Hopkins (12)	103
Hannah Mansfield (12)	103
Paige Sanders (13)	104
Victoria Hardy (12)	105
Matthew Baker (12)	105
Hannah Cornford (13)	106
Cate Welmers (12)	106
Sophie Romain (12)	107
Sam Crow (13)	108
Joseph Lee (12)	108
Zack Weekes (12)	109
Tom Child (11)	109

The Poems

The Thai Jungle

I can hear the distant screams and howls of the animals
Tucked away invisibly in the deep
Hidden in the depths of the mangled and overgrown jungle
I hear the rustling and breathing of animals asleep.

In the silent wind I can see the trees swaying
As if they were dancing uncontrollably
I see the monkeys jumping from tree to tree
Like acrobats in the air, playing.

I can feel the rough twisted trees
Tied together like string
I can feel the smooth umbrella-like leaves
Shading my head from the dazzling sun
Like an angel with wings.

The humidity is oppressive and overpowering with its smells
But, I like being in the jungle
To hear the story that it tells.

Isabella Bailey (11)

If Only

If only there was no pollution floating through the air
If only people would stop, listen and then try to care
If only we could fix the problems in the world today
And then instead of saying stop, we would say OK.

If only there was no corruption on the Planet Earth
People would admire magical things like birth
If only animals wouldn't die from a bullet in the brain
And more people wouldn't use cars, planes or trains.

If only poverty wasn't a problem in the economy
And people would help others if they fall and graze their knee
If only all these problems were not here today
And then instead of saying stop, we would say OK.

Jacob Endicott (13)
Ashton Park School, Bristol

Recycling Starts Now!

You drink from a can and throw it out
Not before knowing what recycling's about
You read the paper and recycle it too
You may also recycle any old shoes.

You collect all the bottles, dispose of the waste
With all that cardboard, for food that you taste
Recycling saves a great deal of time
You recycle those bottles, once filled with wine.

You find something old and make it anew
Nothing is false but all of it's true
With plastic bags to use every day
Which people may use in a lot of ways.

So join the nation and join all in hands
Start in your home and through all the land
Save your things to recycle one day
So work together and make sure recycling stays.

Jamie Mills (14)
Ashton Park School, Bristol

Pollution

The smoke from factories everywhere
Suffocating our nice clean air
The thick pollution filling the city streets
The putrid gas gives us the creeps.

Sickly smog in the sky
Choking the people passing by
Black fog coughing out of the cars' exhausts
Black oil infecting the sea's shores.

Make sure our city is clean
Make sure our world is green
With your help pollution will be a thing of the past
This world has got to last.

Matthew Prosser (13)
Ashton Park School, Bristol

Homeless

The damp concrete pavements my rest for tonight
Dangerous in the day, secure in the night
Helplessly alone with no one to care
The streets busy and full, but really no one's there.

The hard stone pavements are my bed, solid and cold
Greasy papers support my head, smothered in mould
Car horns and buskers, music to my ears
Public melodies for everyone, but for only me to hear.

A thoughtless round coin, thrown in my direction
My simply paid wage and my scandalous reflection
My thoughts and questions, is this really my life?
Regrets cut me like a feared and killer knife.

Walking around on shoes made of skin
Blistered and slaughtered by shards of can and tin
Straggly hair, torn and battered clothes
I'm just the man that everybody loathes.

Tyler Curtis (13)
Ashton Park School, Bristol

Stop The Chop!

Chop, chop, choppity-chop, chop, chop away
Folks in Brazil hear that all day
Chop, chop, choppity-chop, the business must come first
Leave the loggers off for best and forests off for worse.

Chop, chop, choppity-chop, they're cutting down the trees
Running away from the woods are birds, bats and bees
Chop, chop, choppity-chop, the forests are to go
Space after empty space, where trees stood in a row.

Chop, chop, choppity-chop, but plant another seed
This is how it should work, businessmen take heed
Chop, chop, choppity-chop, buy your sustainable goods
Leaving to grow once again a healthy, happy wood.

Jacob Hopkins (13)
Ashton Park School, Bristol

Why?

I am a child soldier
My gun is bigger than me
I have killed 1,000 people
And I am only 13.

The people say we are fighting for freedom
But from what I've seen
It only means death
I beg of you
With my tears and fears
Let me free and be happy again
The Lord has abandoned us
Left us to rot
In the hands of death
Let me see my parents
Let me see my brother
Let me see my village
Oh my God, we destroyed it all
Why?

Malin White (13)
Ashton Park School, Bristol

War

The war is a bore
A bore is the war
If we have more wars
We get more bores!

A gun is not fun
Fun is not a gun
If we got a gun
We get less fun.

The war is a bore
A gun is not fun
We want more fun
We don't want more bore!

Josh Bickley (13)
Ashton Park School, Bristol

Ever Wondered

Ever wonder what the world will be like in 100 years or so?
Will it continue to grow?
One thing's for sure though
Whatever happens, we're there through it all
I mean think about it
Life's not perfect, neither is anyone in it
Therefore, the Earth isn't either
And you know why?
It's because of us
All the pollution in the air
The melting ice caps, the poor polar bears
The torrential rainstorms
The rising rivers
Terrible flooding of our towns
Will it stop and will we all drown?

Ellie Horler (13)
Ashton Park School, Bristol

Private Duty

On duty there are:
Men fighting in the war
Fighting to regain the law
Hoping to patch up the flaw
Trying to find the war's core
In his heart he is torn
Hoping to stop the bloody war
Trying to fight for suffering poor
Trying to stop the conflict for
All the bloodshed he has seen
Waiting for home even more
Trying to find a way for sure
For his family who he hasn't seen
Will this country find the law?
Will families be reunited?
Will hope be re-lighted?

Thomas Case (13)
Ashton Park School, Bristol

How To Save The World

Ever wondered what would happen in 100 years or so?
Whether the planet dies or will it continue to grow?
Well read on and find out how you could stop the world dying
Slow down global warming, slow down the world drying.

First of all, walk or cycle to school
Don't get driven, use that new bike you've been given
Another helpful thing, turn down the central heating by one degree
And maybe volunteer for an environmental charity.

The next thing is remember to recycle
It doesn't take that long
Ending up in landfill sites is where they don't belong.

Don't take a long deep bath
Have a quick shower
So you're never hogging the bathroom for more than an hour.

Take an interest in environmental issues
Though some are quite upsetting, so pass the tissues.

So there are some ideas on how *you* can keep the world happy and healthy
Plus all these ideas don't cost that much,
So you don't have to be too wealthy.

Bala Piti (13)
Ashton Park School, Bristol

Have You!

Have you ever seen a monkey swing from tree to tree?
Have you ever seen a cheetah run so happily?
Have you ever seen a kangaroo jump so excitedly?
Soon this will be over because we have not helped so easily
So these animals will be forgotten in years to come
Because of this planet we will have made them extinct.

Jessica Ash (12)
Ashton Park School, Bristol

What A Wonderful World

(Rewritten from the original 'What A Wonderful World' by Louis Armstrong)

I see trees chopped down, dead roses too
Wilting and dying because of me and you
And I think to myself . . .
Once this was a wonderful world.

I see skies of grey and clouds of smoke
It's supposed to be summer, is this supposed to be a joke?
And I think to myself . . .
Once this was a wonderful world.

The colours of the rainbow fade to soot in the sky
Reflected horror on the faces of people going by
I see wars being fought, mothers crying without a clue
That this didn't have to happen . . . we used to love you.

I hear babies crying from the heat in the air
They'll learn one day, it is 'cause no one cared
And I think to myself . . .
Once this was a wonderful world.

The colours of the rainbow fade to soot in the sky
Reflected horror on the faces of people going by
I see wars being fought, mothers crying without a clue
This didn't have to happen . . . we used to love you.

I hear babies crying from the heat in the air
They'll learn one day it's 'cause no one cared
And I say let's go and make this . . . a wonderful world
Yes, I say let's go restore this . . . to a wonderful world.

Frederica Drewer (13)
Ashton Park School, Bristol

How To Save The World!

If Superman and Spider-Man come flying through the air
Then we should be able to save the world in a way that's only fair!
For global warming is no trick and pollution surfs the sky
We'll have to solve these problems, fast and slick but not just you and I.

The world's a very crowded place, we'll need a helping hand
If we want to save the human race, they'll have to understand . . .
So broadcast on the television, any way to let them know
To pick their litter off the ground and in the bin it goes.

And only take one bath a year, but showers all the rest
Especially if you make it clear, less water used is best
The ice caps are melting quickly, save the polar bear
So remember when you drive your cars the world is ours to share.

Next time you think of Superman and all the good he does
Try to do the best you can to stop the world go *bust!*

Gracie Martin (13)
Ashton Park School, Bristol

Red Rose

People lying on the floor
Guns blazing through the mist
People targeting you through the moor
Always looking down the list.

Machine guns blaring under the sun
Armed tanks surging through the fields
Nothing stops until the job's done
Both armies without their shields.

Everyone wearing their bright red roses
Men wearing suits rented from the shop
People standing tall, making poses
The motto was, don't stop till you drop.

Lewis Smart (14)
Ashton Park School, Bristol

Untitled

I was born in the gutter
And I never got out
I live in a rich country
But I live in doubt.

People look down on me
Stand on me and spit on me
People think I'm scum
Just because I'm a bum.

What can we do?
What can we say?
If we take the time to think
We can save a bum today.

Daisy Brickwell & Georgia Burgess (13)
Ashton Park School, Bristol

Poverty

No water, no food
Lost family, even dead
Orphan children, no parents
All because of poverty.

Children working for pennies
In every kind of weather
Dirty water is a treat
All because of poverty.

People homeless and dying
With all sorts of diseases
They have no life
All because of poverty.

Melissa Eddolls (13)
Ashton Park School, Bristol

War

War turns men into beasts
War kills the man
War kills the land
War tears the land.

War has only darkness
War has no justice
War has no laws
War has no peace.

War creates greed
War is the source of sins
War creates fear
War creates destruction.

Jordan Williams (14)
Ashton Park School, Bristol

War

War tears the land
War kills the land
War kills the man
War turns men into beasts.

War has no law
War has no justice
War has no peace
War has only darkness.

War causes fear
War creates destruction
War creates greed
War is a source of sins.

Kyle Tadawan (14)
Ashton Park School, Bristol

How To Save The World

This world is not our home
We are just passing by
Yet on our way we are slowly destroying it
Our minds are somewhere else
Somewhere beyond the seas
We do not have the time
To waste with stupid things
Like war and racism
Litter and pollution
So stop these stupid things
And help to save the world
Or like many other things
We will be unseen and unknown.

Sophie Longhurst (14)
Ashton Park School, Bristol

Racism

Lots of things are black and white
Why be racist day and night?
People say don't judge a book by its cover
So why do you judge a human by its colour?

If you're a racist it will haunt you
Put yourself in the victim's shoes
It will daunt you.

Don't judge the colour of someone's skin
It is wrong, it is a sin
You take pictures in black and white
If you're a racist you'll get a fright.

Sophie Backwell (14)
Ashton Park School, Bristol

Kind Man

Kind man loves rainforests
He hates pollution, poverty, racism
War and litter
He cares for the homeless and animals
He recycles everything
And stops this climate change
By walking and biking
Oh kind man!

Jak Derrick (13)
Ashton Park School, Bristol

Recycle

R ecycle your rubbish
E very day
C lean your planet in every way
Y ou can recycle old paper
C ans and bottles too
L itter is a bad thing
E very day is a new.

Holly Templar (13)
Ashton Park School, Bristol

Recycle

R ecycle
E very
C an
Y ou
C onsume.
L ove the
E nvironment.

Lucy Reed (13)
Ashton Park School, Bristol

Walking To School

You see mums talking about
While little kids scream and shout
Mums and dads driving around
before finding that quiet sound
All you see is newly built flats
Goodbye to all those old built pubs
Being replaced with flats and clubs
Saying goodbye to those happy memories.

Imogen Parry (14)
Ashton Park School, Bristol

My Message

Recycling, it's the new trend
'I turn off my lights, I'm so green!'
'I never watch telly, I'm so eco-active!'
But why? What does it all mean?

Do we recycle to be cool?
Do we recycle just so we can brag about it?
Or do we do it to help change,
And save our planet?

Our world is brill
Light at the flick of a thumb
But we could make a big difference by switching off
And save loads of money for Dad and Mum.

Imagine no polar bears
No river Thames or Congo
No glorious mountains standing tall,
No eerie icebergs covered in snow.

My message is a simple one
Extremely easy to understand
Go green - recycle!
For the Earth's existence is in our hands.

Grace Crowley (13)
Beaulieu Convent School, Jersey

A Bigger Price

They banned carrier bags just last week
The adults moan about the price, 'cause it's not cheap.
'5p for a bag, what an expense!'
So buy a reusable one, stop being so tense
'Supermarket prices, just go up and up!'
They wouldn't if the ozone layer started closing up!

Above Australia is where the hole is open
Where we get our wheat, the prices aren't frozen
The UV rays burning out, the crops and the land
Making wheat scarce, the price's the demand.

'Petrol . . . extortionate, they're trying to rip us off!'
Stop using it up, they hear me scoff
'The traffic's terrible, how to avoid it?'
By walking or cycling, time to get fit.

'Those poor people in Africa, they're so needy!'
It's the sun again, so stop being so greedy
They fight over oil as it's running out
This causes war with this is no doubt.

The island I live on is estimated to be
In two hundred years time, under the sea
It won't affect the adults, they won't be here
Our generations in two hundred years.

If we all do our part you can see
How helpful recycling can really be
But everyone thinks the environment won't change
With a little bit of effort time will rearrange.

The way we live today and tomorrow
Reusable resources are there to borrow
I could go on forever telling you what to do
But this right now is our cue.

They banned carriers bags just last week
The adults moan about the price, 'cause it's not cheap
But when you read this I want you to realise
The fate of other's lives is a bigger price.

Tamarah Green (12)
Beaulieu Convent School, Jersey

Reduce Pollution

We have to learn to recycle
To keep our Earth clean
So don't throw your rubbish
To the planet, that is mean.

The cars are polluting
And so are the trains,
Your electrical appliances
Plugged into the mains.

The factories are doing it
And the ships on the sea,
When rooms are pitch-black
You don't use electricity.

We have to remember to stay green
Reduce our carbon footprint
And then you will see
A cleaner world, a cleaner home,
A nicer place to live and grow.

Tobias Chilton (12)
Brune Park Community School, Gosport

Pollution

P aper is our trees, our oxygen
O ur world, our problem
L ions will become extinct
L aughter will soon die
U se roll-ons, not aerosols
T rees are disappearing
I ce melting
O ur Earth is dying
N ow stop polluting!

Louise Hunt (12)
Brune Park Community School, Gosport

Save The World

Many different gases fill the air
This isn't really fair
How could we let it get like this?
Our world should be full of bliss.

You should start to recycle
Stop the car and use a bicycle
Turn off your light
It'll save a world fight.

Help clean our Earth
Like it was at birth
The world should be green
So stop being so mean.

No one wants to know
So we have to show
That we do care
So stop polluting the air.

Becky Lees (15)
Brune Park Community School, Gosport

What Is Happening? Pollution!

Smoke is billowing from dark, dirty factories
It's polluted smoke
Cans, bottles and paper
Rubbish is scattered around
I see it everywhere
I can always hear
Clink rustle, snap, bang, shuffle
Rolling and rotting
What is happening?
I think to myself sadly
Pollution is here
But it shouldn't be!

Caitlin Martin (12)
Brune Park Community School, Gosport

What Does The Word Mean To You?

The word pollution means what to you?
Over the years the world has become full of CO_2.
Recycle your paper and glass, turn old to new,
The world needs not one, not two, but a few.
Streets are full of rubbish due to you.
People need to use a bike not four wheels but two.

Global warming is killing the world today,
We have not got any time to play,
Get your bike out, use your legs, you hear me say,
It's time to make a difference today.

All the rubbish and CO_2 is causing pollution,
There is no easy solution,
But I have a conclusion,
So help me and the rest of the world,
To sort out this pollution,
We need a solution.

Natalie Skilton (15)
Brune Park Community School, Gosport

The Future Is In Our Hands

Pollution is all around us
In the air, on the TV and the radio
Every piece of litter you dump
Contributes to your carbon footprint
The future is in our hands.

In 30 years time
The whole world could be under water
More and more natural disasters happening
Every day the whole world destroyed
People living in what's left of their homes
Living in fear for their own lives
We have the power to change it now
The future is in our hands.

Aisling Morrissey (12)
Brune Park Community School, Gosport

Pollution Kills, Kills You

Pollution is our world today, horrible and bad
Children can't go out to play, that is so sad.

Gas fires, electric and rubbish too
Humans and animals all release poo.

Rainforests, tree extinction, dark clouds too
All cause pollution that kills you.

The sun which causes melting ice
Also burps and pops aren't very nice.

Phones and communities waste the carbon footprint
Stop using cars and do a sprint.

The Ice Age is bad so is cargo and oil
Fumes and aerosols make the world boil.

Solar panels, factories are as bad as smog
Smog is just bigger and thicker fog.

The list that I've written for you are things that cause pollution
Follow the rules, stop the pollution
It's coming, coming to kill, kill you!

Sabrina Marshall & Chloe Hearnden-Hayes (12)
Brune Park Community School, Gosport

Save The World

       P   eople littering pollutes our world
   V O lcanoes erupt because of pollution
Recyc L   e our rubbish to save the world
       L   et's join together to save the planet
       U   nder water is the same
       T   reat our Earth with care or
   An I   ce Age will come
   N O warnings there will be
    I N the end you will freeze!

Ryan Evans (12)
Brune Park Community School, Gosport

The Pain Of The People's Vain

There has to be a solution
To stop this horrible pollution
Or else all that we have made
Will come to its conclusion.

These things that help us so
Will cause us all to go
We think we are all right
But there is nothing we can show.

All this nuclear waste
Will cause us all to face
The future that will not come
For our children all to paste.

There is a way to the light
To be able to make things right
The world's future is in peril
To all of the pollution's height.

Harry Stroud (15)
Brune Park Community School, Gosport

Our World's Solution

We used to be fine
Working on the vines
When we'd walk to buy our wine

When bicycles were the craze
When a fast car didn't waste your days
When all you did was bathe

But now there's no solution
For all of our pollution
So I draw to my conclusion

What's your clever solution
To our planet full of pollution?

Stephanie Hoskins (15)
Brune Park Community School, Gosport

Rap For Life

Pollution is bad
And we do the most
We need to stop
For the living of Earth.

Burning of trees
Dropping of litter
Stop right now
So you don't turn bitter.

Walk or run
On your feet
Don't drive your car
Or you'll lose your beat.

Pollution is bad
And we do the most.

Jade Wilson (12)
Brune Park Community School, Gosport

Untitled

Pollution is bad
It is very sad
Trees are going down
It's not sound.

Storms are coming
People are running
Our air is dirty
But not flirty.

Factories ruin the world
Carbon dioxide swirls
Extinction is arriving
Animals are dying.

Save our world or you'll die!

Leah Duery (11)
Brune Park Community School, Gosport

Our Solution

Pollution is bad
Pollution is cruel
It makes people sad
So let's rise up tall
Let's stop pollution
And rise with a solution.

Use your bike
Or even take a hike
There are ways to stop pollution
So listen to my solution
Don't use your car
To get to the bar
Use your feet
And stick to the beat.

Let's stop pollution
And rise with a solution
Let's all come together
And all sing forever
Let's stop pollution
Then we have our solution.

Kayleigh White (15)
Brune Park Community School, Gosport

Pollution

Pollution is bad
It makes people sad
You only need a car
To drive really far
Or maybe a plane
If you wanna go to Spain
Use your bike
But not your car
Pollution is bad
It makes people sad!

Amy Carlisle (12)
Brune Park Community School, Gosport

We Can Save Our World!

There are many ways to stop pollution
So why don't we start now
If everyone puts some effort in
Stop it, yes we shall.

If we all recycle
And yes, I know we can
Instead of using petrol
We could cycle down the town.

Our seas will never be the same
With all the rubbish in them
So if we all use litter bins
There'll be none there again.

So if we stop pollution
The world will be a better place
Then we'll all be happy
And the world will be ace!

Rhiannon Winstanley (11)
Brune Park Community School, Gosport

Global Warming

The world is being polluted
Everyone dropping litter
Global warming is it a threat?
Fumes all around us
Cars everywhere
Rainforests being chopped down
Animals becoming extinct
Global warming is it a threat?
Factories puffing out smoke
Greenhouse gases
Help us! Do you want to live?

Charlotte Moore (12)
Brune Park Community School, Gosport

Saving The World

The more we use electricity
The more we damage the land
Global warming is arriving
So give the world a hand.

Think of all the penguins
And all the polar bears
These animals are dying
But no one seems to care.

To stop this all from happening
Recycle all your goods
Turn off objects you're not using
This saves trees or even woods.

Motorbikes, cars and lorries
Are giving off lots of gas
So why not ride a bicycle
This will decrease the mass?

By helping just a little
You're learning quite a lot
So start from right this second
Pollution will be gone like a shot.

Amy Roberts (14)
Brune Park Community School, Gosport

Pollution Is Bad

Factory smoke is really bad
It makes people choke
And makes them sad
If you want to use a car
You can use it, but not too far
Do not use a mobile phone
Because it makes a really bad tone.

Erin Atkinson (11)
Brune Park Community School, Gosport

The Clouds Of The Planet

In the clouds of the planet
Little children cry over their beautiful sky
Where the clouds of the planet
Have poisoned the sky.

In the clouds of the planet
The trees began to weep
Where the clouds of the planet
Burn their souls.

In the clouds of the planet
The heat begins to rise
Where the clouds of the planet
Warm up the hate inside.

In the clouds of the planet
The fuel begins to die
Where the clouds of the planet
Runs down the fuel.

In the clouds of the planet
Man begins to fight
Where the clouds of the planet
Feeds Man's greed.

So in the clouds of the planet
Will end us all . . .

Jason Mills (15)
Brune Park Community School, Gosport

Energy Savers

E co-friendly people
N ever let the world down
E very day they save us energy
R eady to be wasted the next day
G enerating energy is killing our planet
Y ou can make a difference, start to save today.

Daisy Wyatt (12)
Brune Park Community School, Gosport

Get Rid Of It!

Pollution is here
Pollution is there
Pollution is everywhere!

Dropping of litter
And burning of trees
If you don't be careful
We'll lose our bees.

That means no flowers
And no *air*
We definitely all know
That wouldn't be fair.

Pollution is here
Pollution is there
Pollution is everywhere
So get rid of it!

Ria Chaston (11)
Brune Park Community School, Gosport

Meltdown

Polar bears are dying
Because they have no homes
So help them with their lifestyle
Or they'll be skin and bones.

The Earth is getting hotter
The ozone is getting thin
This means the ice is melting
To me this is a sin.

So start by being careful
With everything you use
Electricity and energy is precious
Pollution is now becoming abuse!

Rosanna Chilvers (15)
Brune Park Community School, Gosport

Saving Our Planet

We can save our planet every day
So get out of your cars and walk the way
Smell the air and feel so proud of what you have done
You helped save the world everyone
So help us clean up your ways
To keep the world safe for all our sakes
You can have fun all the way
If you are in a hurry, grab a bike and cycle all the way
You can do it every day
So do it while there's still time
To make a difference like it says in my rhyme!

Natasha Sylvester (12)
Brune Park Community School, Gosport

What Is Pollution?

What is pollution?
Pollution is around us everywhere
Not that people really care
Wouldn't it be nice to have clean air?

Has anyone heard of global warming?
We should take this as more of a warning
And one day wake up to a nice clean morning.

I think for pollution there is no solution
We should switch to green and keep the world clean.

Alex O'Neill (15)
Brune Park Community School, Gosport

I Wish . . .

I wish . . .
I had something that I could give to all the homeless people
Who have nowhere to live
Do they deserve to live this way?
With at least one child dying each and every day?
In the Third World countries, it's becoming a disaster
Dangerous diseases spreading even faster
Sometimes it really makes me think
How do they survive with so little to drink?
At least one child dies every day
Do they really deserve to live this way?
I wish every child had a smile on their face
It would make the world a more pleasant place.

Vicky Culbertson
Chamberlayne Park School, Southampton

Tears Of The Government

He sat at the doorway of 100 sorrows
Where the war on poverty will always follow
He says to himself what shall he do?
When the war with Afghanistan is almost through
He dreams of freedom in the countryside
Where the red kite will peacefully glide
He wishes that songs will be sung
And that freedom to people will be brought
We shall rejoice with the loudest of voices
We all shall make our biggest choices.

Reece Alexander (15)
Chamberlayne Park School, Southampton

How Long Will It Last?

The world was green, full of life
No pollution and still had light
Then Man came and shook the Earth
Trees cut down, factories giving birth.

The world kept spinning as things got worse
Deep underground things began to burst
Through day to night, houses were planted
Population grew and rubbish mounted.

The world's no bigger than when we began
We need some improvements to plan
We want this light to stay light
How long will it last?

Rachel Carter (14) & Amy Blackman (14)
Chamberlayne Park School, Southampton

Global Warming

G lowing embers
L osing the Earth
O ur time to shine
B lackening coal
A nother emergency hits Earth
L ight is fading day by day

W e only live once
A ll together now
R eading the signs
M ums and dads helping
I ndigo skies burn the coast
N o time to lose time to
G o!

Daniel Fry (14)
Chamberlayne Park School, Southampton

Help Change The World!

Walk or cycle, instead of a car
It might take longer, to get as far
But a little difference could make a big change
You can change the world, so why not do it today?
When you go shopping, reuse plastic bags
Bags for life are sure to last.

Help the poor and buy Fair Trade
It may cost more, but they're getting better pay
So listen up to what I say
You can change the world
So start today!

Jodie Trevatt (14)
Chamberlayne Park School, Southampton

Rubbish

The world is a ball of rubbish
With its crime and people who are sluggish
And its racism, terrorism and war
But on top of that no one cares for the poor.

So what can we do?
Oh, you can help too
We will clean up the shore
Or visit the poor
And help out with the law.

And after that
The world will be a better place to live
To love and to dump our waste.

Joshua Bosley (13)
Chamberlayne Park School, Southampton

Environmental Health

E very place has been polluted
N owhere is safe
V arious causes of destruction
I f you help you can make a difference
R ich people are causing poverty
O nly you can make a difference
N ow is the time to take drastic action
M ore deaths are caused because of pollution
E veryone can change our environment
N ow pollution is killing our planet
T ime to change
A nyone could change the world
L ife in the environment needs saving

H ope is needed
E arth should be a great place to live in
A nimals are dying
L ife needs to be saved
T ake control
H elp save our environment.

Amy Jefferey (13)
Chamberlayne Park School, Southampton

The World Is Slowly Dying

The world is slowly dying
All around people are crying
The sky is falling all around
If we clean it up
It will be fun
Everyone gather around
And help clean up with gloves.

Shannon Filgate (11)
Chamberlayne Park School, Southampton

It's Got To Stop

It's got to stop
I tell you
It's got to stop
Everyone should be equal
No matter the colour of your skin
Everyone should be equal.

There is a split through the middle
But really people should mingle
Skin, hair, race
No matter what is the case
The bullying should stop
The world would be a better place.

It will get much worse
If no one tries to help
People may get injured
Or worse even killed
It's getting worse by the minute
Read the poster, don't bin it.

It's got to stop
I tell you
It's got to stop!

Katie Tulett (13)
Chamberlayne Park School, Southampton

Rubbish, Rubbish

Rubbish, rubbish everywhere
Soon there will be no room
So even you can recycle
Just to save maybe one tree.

All around the world
People are polluting the world
Day by day
Week by week.

Leanna Clayton (12)
Chamberlayne Park School, Southampton

War Is All Around Us!

War is all around us, no matter where we look
Villages and families destroyed, thousands dead
Wives, mothers, children, fathers, uncles, aunts
Orphaned children litter the streets just looking for a bite to eat
Waiting to die, to enter the abyss, to rest at last from the blood
The bodies, the rubble and the cries
Bangs and crashes, roars of wind, empty shells and bullets
Gases in the air, blood on the floor,
Running like a little stream
People running, crawling home to face destruction and deceit
The horror, the screams, the laughter and the cries, the darkness
and the light
The illness, the dying, the pain and dislike
Day by day, night by night, the darkness is getting closer
The world is what we make it and everywhere is different.

Jessica Venn (14)
Chamberlayne Park School, Southampton

The Rainforest

Further and further, in you go
No sign of sun, no sign of snow
Until there's light shining on your head
Where are the trees? They're not up ahead
Who would take this life away?
Over and over, day by day . . .
I look around for a clue
With trees like barriers, it feels like a zoo
Monkeys screaming, their home has gone
The only thing is they're not the only ones
There's birds, lizards and even bees too
These poor animals and there's nothing I can do!

Devonne Dewey (13)
Costello College of Technology, Basingstoke

The Sounds Of The Rainforest

The bees buzz, the birds call
The tractor starts, the trees fall
The monkeys scream and run away
They have no home, no place to stay.
The land's flooded, beetles and all
Monkeys stranded in trees so tall
Parrots caw, butterflies flap
What will survive in this man-made trap?
Fish splash, hogs grunt
Knives slash and men hunt
Crocodiles snap, gorillas cry
Their homes are destroyed with a heavy sigh
What will be there after the men have left?
The rainforest's not theirs, this must be theft
Piranhas bite, tree rats squeak
Where are the ancient remedies we used to seek?
What will be left for our children tomorrow?
Silence in the rainforest and hearts full of sorrow
The bees don't buzz, the birds don't call
The tractors stops and no trees fall
There's silence in the ashes, silence on the ground
Silence in the skies, no animals to be found
All the trees are gone now, no nutrients in the earth
We have to replant the trees, lay down the brand new turf
They'll never know the snaps, squeaks or grunting
At least the men will stop hunting
The only sound you'll hear is the shouting tourist
Because there is no sound left in the forest
All there is, is silence!

Sarah Budge (13)
Costello College of Technology, Basingstoke

Racism

Whether you're black
Whether you're white
It doesn't really matter
As they are both right.

You laugh about my colour
Hit me, tease and shout
You make me tell my mother
But I still have my doubts.

There's nothing I can do about it
Just please stop it now
I feel like I just wanna cry
I even want to shout.

This is how you make me feel
How can you think it's right?
Please just leave me alone for once
Without giving me a fright.

I think of all the others
That go through this each day
Why don't you just leave us
And treat us all the same?

Laura-Jane Wrey (13)
Costello College of Technology, Basingstoke

Do It Cleaner, Make It Greener

So come on now, there's not much time
Act now, all will be fine
We need to recycle more
And if you don't, I'll be at your door.

What must be done, must be done
This war needs to be won.

Martin Smith (12)
Costello College of Technology, Basingstoke

One World

One world, one chance
That's all we've got
Cut it and it's gone

Day by day
It's a massacre of the hundreds
Your only friend, the tree, dead

My view is endless
I see the doom, falling upon us
I hear a wailing noise

Death is all I see
My world dying
Falling trees all the time

Stop!
Give us a chance
To help to clear up

Your mess is killing the lost
Stop your sins, stop the misdeeds
Our life is about to end.

Vignesh Piramanayagam (12)
Costello College of Technology, Basingstoke

Recycling

By 2030 the world will be brown
Yes brown, like the rubbish we dump down
So open the big green bin
And dump recyclables in
That will make the world far better
Also by reusing all old letters
So in 2030 the world won't break apart
As long as you get up and do your part.

Angel Lynch (11)
Costello College of Technology, Basingstoke

If The World Was A Better Place

If the world was a better place
The oceans would be cleared from dumping
The poverty-stricken would have money to spare
And the rainforests would be in full bloom.

If the world was a better place
All races would be equal
Conflict would be banned
And peace would be found.

As the world is today
War rages in Iraq
Waters are polluted
And racism continues
It has to stop!

Cavan Reid (11)
Costello College of Technology, Basingstoke

People In Poverty

No one is there to hear their cry
More and more are to die
They have no food and no water
They go to work, it's just slaughter
They have no life, no place to stay
They wish their pain would go away
Large families on the street
Begging for food still on their feet
Poverty is worldwide
But people just put it aside
No one cares what they feel
Day to day they search for meals
We take advantage of what we get
While they sit outside getting wet
How they feel we shouldn't forget
Help today, so there's no regrets!

Lenina Rogerson (12)
Costello College of Technology, Basingstoke

Do We Need This Destruction?

The pull of a trigger
From a heartless man
Ends an animal's life
But they don't give a damn.

Some call it sport
Others call it cruel
But the animals still die
And the blood still pools.

Forests are cut down
For farming and money
They grow smaller and smaller
Yet more find the matter funny.

The answer to this problem is simple
Leave the animals alone
The only reason to kill them is greed, fear and pleasure
Tell me, are they good reasons?

Samuel Hennem (11)
Costello College of Technology, Basingstoke

Think

Think of yourself as a polar bear
How does it feel to live with fear?
Always scared that you'll die very soon
Sitting down, terrified, staring at the moon
The sun shines and they burn
A weather that they can't turn
Their ice changes into water
They are homeless and have no shelter
If you just save electricity, it can help a lot
Poor polar bears can't live in weather so hot
So please, do your bit to help!

Sarina Gurung (12)
Costello College of Technology, Basingstoke

Pollution

P reparing for the destruction of the Earth
O ld and grey the air is becoming
L ots of sun
L ots of rain
U gh, will it ever be normal again?
T iny drops of water and hail
I n and out of the dark black clouds
O n the clock the hours passed
N ow the Earth is flooding.

Stan Rhys Brown (12)
Costello College of Technology, Basingstoke

Racism

I don't really see why people fight
About the colours, black and white
We are all the same, I see no right
When all sad people choose to fight
They've done no wrong, what's the matter?
It's not because England's getting fatter
They're coming here to make amends
So please just be some decent men!

Serené Adams (12)
Costello College of Technology, Basingstoke

Litter

Dropping your rubbish is very bad
It's making people very sad
The rubbish you drop will make pollution worse
So just put your rubbish in the bin
It can help global warming
Save the world from never dawning!

Chloë Aldcroft (12)
Costello College of Technology, Basingstoke

Litter

Litter is bad and makes people sad
It smells a lot and wrecks a plot
So when you buy a can of pop
Don't walk along and then drop
If you see a bit of litter on the floor
Pick it up and shut the bin door
Don't drop litter anymore.

Amelia Colegate (12)
Costello College of Technology, Basingstoke

What Am I?

There used to be many of us
But now only a few
I feel so lonely with nothing to do
We were all OK until they came
They came with guns and machines
I run as fast as I can
Trying to get away
Why can't they leave us alone?
Soon will all be gone.

Darryl Packman (12)
Cove School, Farnborough

Waves - Haiku

Waves raising up high
Flooding a lot of places
Families upset.

Charlie Bluck (12)
Cove School, Farnborough

Eco Issues

Recycle plastic, bottles and paper
Recycle card, cans and other metals
We should recycle, it's our world we live in.

Deforestation, what does it mean?
It means not pulling down trees
And not ruining animals' habitats.

Pollution, what can we do to stop it?
Stop throwing oil and rubbish in the seas
Stop dumping and burning cars all over waste ground.

What are the natural disasters?
Earthquakes and hurricanes
Strong winds and flooding.

Melleah Gunn (12)
Cove School, Farnborough

What Am I?

I blaze like the sun
I do what I want
Nothing will stand in my way
But there is just one thing
it makes me cold
It puts me out
But it doesn't take away
The damage I leave
Before I start
There's a few things I need
Friction, oxygen, no need for CO_2
But missing ingredient
Of course, is *you*
To burn with me.

Jade Haley (13)
Cove School, Farnborough

Eco Poem

One day the world will be safe
From the greenhouse gases that we make
Tsunamis, hurricanes, flooding and droughts
Global warming is what these are about.
Plastic bags, litter, deforestation and fires
We need greener energy through our wires
Earthquakes and natural disasters
Caused partly by our industrial masters.
From the pollution in our air and seas
To cutting down too many trees
Our carbon footprint is produced
When power and vehicles are used
This carbon footprint will increase
When it is, we won't be pleased
Act now on CO_2
Or read this poem another time through.

Bradley Porter (13)
Cove School, Farnborough

Deforestation - It Needs To Stop

Green, green trees
Going
Going
Gone!

Holly McLeod (13)
Cove School, Farnborough

Litter - Haiku

Scattered on the floor
Ruining our home, places
Needs to be stopped now!

Jessica Flynn (13)
Cove School, Farnborough

Flooding - Haiku

Floods causes damage
Floods ruin all the houses
Lives are ruining.

Catherine Hunter (13)
Cove School, Farnborough

Racist Abuse

R acism is bad
A nd you could offend someone
C an you stop it?
I t is bad and abusive
S top it *right now!*
T o help people, don't be racist

A busing is very bad
B ecause you can be offensive
U nder *no* circumstances
S hould you be racist
E ven if you are angry with someone
    with a different skin colour to you.

Kayleigh Adams (12)
Hanham High School, Bristol

Homeless

H elpless
O n their own
M oney
E very day
L onely
E ruption of tears
S tarvation
S olitary.

Oliver Adams (11)
Hanham High School, Bristol

Sores And Scratches

My stepdad gives me scratches
And he burns me with matches
If I tell my mother
He said he'd kill my brother
So I end up keeping quiet
But it ends up in a riot
So I called the NSPCC
And now I see the world differently.

Samantha Callaghan (11)
Hanham High School, Bristol

Why War?

Why do we have wars?
Killing people at their doors
Bombs scattered everywhere
As I think how they dare
To cause grief and fright
As they just keep the fight
More and more
And the people feel so sore.

Adam Hulbert (12)
Hanham High School, Bristol

Warfare

W arfare is nasty
A ttackers are horrible
R einforcements are kind
F ighting is very horrible
A ir strikes
R esistance
E vacuation.

Chris Carr (12)
Hanham High School, Bristol

The Climate Change

T ornadoes grow
H urricanes kill
E arthquakes destroy

C ountless people die
L ightning strikes
I ce caps melt
M any more people die
A ll together we cause this
T ogether we must stop
E ventually climate change will happen

C limate change is real
H igh winds blow
A t last it will come
N o more sun
G ets home quick
E ventually it has come.

Ryan Bennett (11)
Hanham High School, Bristol

Share The Love

A nimals left at
N ight, where no one cares
I n the garden all alone
M ight I say they are equivalent to us
A ll they want is
L ove and care

C an they have some love?
R eally they should
U se your brain and don't be cruel
E veryone and everything is equal
L ove them like yourself
T hat's not you, that is them
Y es you should.

Kieran Coles (11)
Hanham High School, Bristol

Because I Know

I am sad
Because I know
People will die
And so will their foe.

I am glad
Because I know
That I have water
And some people don't.

I am thankful
Because I know
That the water here
Is never low.

I am sad
Because I know
People are dying
Because the rivers don't flow.

Chloe Harris (11)
Hanham High School, Bristol

Racism

There are always attacks
On the people who are black
I get hit with a cane
And then they say, 'No pain, no gain.'
But it really hurts
And the bullies are called berks
They lob some cakes
At my ugly face
And then they ask me, 'Why I pray?'
I say it is my belief and my dad's a priest
But then they call me gay
They say go to Hell
Or they'll lock me in a cell.

Ross Liddington (12)
Hanham High School, Bristol

The World That I Dream In

The sunlight glows
While the river flows
In the world that I dream in.

Trees sway side to side
The birds swoop and glide
Here in the world that I dream in.

Now I wake up and I look outside
To find no birds that swoop and glide
And to find no world that I dream in.

Instead in the real world
I find litter that was chucked
And I find dogs' muck
I wish that this world
Was the world that I dream in.

Megan Rossiter (12)
Hanham High School, Bristol

Animals

One day an animal
Next day it could be gone
All because some people are so wrong
Everyone hears, but no one sees
Because they think they're vermin that carry disease.

Cold on its own, scared to be seen
Owners think they're doing nothing wrong
But really they're just plain mean
Someone help these poor creatures
Some people just don't know their amazing features.

Kayleigh Rimell (12)
Hanham High School, Bristol

Polluting The World

Stop, stop
You're polluting the world
By cutting down trees
And using your cars
Stop, stop
Why can't you stop?
You could start to recycle
Walk or cycle
And help the world to survive.

Stop, stop
The people in Africa
Are all dying
Because they don't have food or drink
Stop, stop
Give them a bit
Of the money
That you have too much of.

Adam Hills (11)
Hanham High School, Bristol

Stop The War!

Stop the wars
We're not nice to the poor
Let them have some mercy

Stop the wars
It's not nice for us
We're in pain
Because every day
We get hit by a flame.

Some people are bad
That makes us sad
But we are glad
That they haven't attacked.

Matthew Sully (11)
Hanham High School, Bristol

Pollution . . . Clean It Up!

Pollution is like tearing our world apart
It's not colourful or pretty, it's definitely not art
Pollution is everywhere, in our streets and in our rivers
The sight of it just gives me the shivers
I wish the madness would eventually stop
Our world is going to blow up one day . . .*pop, pop, pop!*
So do something about it and make the world right
Let everyone see the world, it's a beautiful sight!

Jack Hussey (12)
Hanham High School, Bristol

Suffering Child Abuse

In this world there is so much suffering
Like a kid not knowing what an adult is saying
But no one knows how much pain
You cause the boys and girls in this world
For other people's sick pleasure
They don't deserve this pain, they are put through
But one day hopefully the world will understand which is true.

Rhian Stowell (12)
Hanham High School, Bristol

Summer Gardens

Flowers grow as piles of litter from bins
It gets blown around in the mild breeze
It flies along like an upset storm
Can you make a difference,
Please, please?

Jessica Purnell (12)
Hanham High School, Bristol

World Peace

W ar should have never come, it should be gone
O f course we want world peace instead of being obese
R IP should not be
L ying is worse than dying, so don't
D umping rubbish is very rubbish, very rubbish indeed

P eace should overcome the world
E ven though violence rules
A nd all bullying should die
C lapping and applauding people's good efforts
E veryone should have *peace!*

Josh Owen (12)
Hanham High School, Bristol

Litter

Litter makes a lot of mess
It can cause lots of stress
It makes the world smell very bad
It's making this great planet sad
If we don't take action whilst we can
We'll end up looking like Jupiter
That's not the plan.

Megan Rouch (12)
Hanham High School, Bristol

Cancer

C an't be cured
A nd
N ot rare
C ancer kills
E veryone who has it will
R IP!

Adam Jukes (11)
Hanham High School, Bristol

Racism Matters

Just because they're different
In fact they are the same
They're just the same as you and me
And yet you give them pain.

They are sick of being treated this way
Every time you look and see
You turn your face away.

Because they're a different colour
You tease and hit them too
You never look to see the love
That is in front of you.

So today think of your actions
Before you tease in spite
For our future will always be
Black and white, unite!

Georgie Taylor (12)
Hanham High School, Bristol

Animal Cruelty

Animal cruelty is a shame
But my owner is to blame
She smacks me and whips me every day
She doesn't let me go out to play
Other animals have such a good life
But my life is on the end of a knife
But we're OK
She gave me a kiss
And that gave me a feeling
I really did miss!

Emma Bindon (11)
Hanham High School, Bristol

Nothing's Fair

Being homeless isn't fair
People look and people stare
Should I laugh or should I care?

I want a home to have a bath
To have a bath with bubble foam
All I ask is for a shed
Or maybe a flat with a bed
All I need is to be fed.

I need somewhere to rest in peace
Away from being moved by police
Do I find my brother or do I find my niece?

Being homeless isn't fair
I'm sick and tired of being bare
Should I cry or should I care?

Courtney Eickhoff (12)
Hanham High School, Bristol

Let Them Live In Peace!

People crying like the wind in the night
Their homes are gone just like their lives
Nothing to see, nowhere to go
Just in their dreams, the rivers flow.

Pollution and litter everywhere
It will kill the birds and a big brown bear
Show some appreciation
For our next generation.

People treat them different
But they are just the same
Instead of treating them with respect
We fill their lives with pain.

Charlotte Godwin (12)
Hanham High School, Bristol

Animal Cruelty

Animal cruelty is a shame
But my owner is to blame
She hits me, whips me with a cane.

I live in hurt and wonder
If anyone will come and save me?
I wish and wish every day
For this pain to go away.

I sometimes wish I'm dead
But then I say that it is all just in my head.

Danielle Davey (12)
Hanham High School, Bristol

Killing

K illing sucks
I t's not right
L istening to people suffer
L oud, then quiet
I t is not nice
N ight falls
G rowing up with killing is wrong.

Kieran Hynam (12)
Hanham High School, Bristol

Travel

T he fuel is bad
R ips apart the planet
A ll the fumes
V illains use
E very car driven
L et it know in Heaven.

Bradley Paisey (12)
Hanham High School, Bristol

The River Won't Flow

Tonight I sit and cry
Because I know
My friends will die
as the river won't flow.

We cannot eat
As the crops won't grow
The crops won't grow
As the river won't flow.

We need help
Some food or water please
We need some food or water
So we can live with ease.

Help us, help us, help us, please!

Ellie Haskins (12)
Hanham High School, Bristol

War Is Bad

War is bad
War is stupid
War is many things
But war does not bring peace
War brings destruction
Why have war?
That is what I want to know
War is bad
War is stupid
So why?
Why fight?
That is what I want to know.

Daniel Kendall (11)
Hanham High School, Bristol

No Water Came!

Today I am sad
Because tomorrow I know
My friends will die
I sit in woe
But I am also glad
For all the good times I have had
I remember how we splashed and played
And every night I prayed
That every day would be the same
But it has not and no water has come
People write to ask for food
Which puts people in a mood
As we have no food to spare
And I sit in despair.

Katrina Zalokoski (12)
Hanham High School, Bristol

War, War

War is like giving up
Giving in to the horrible people who fight
Like letting you die in a bin
No matter how big, or what height
You cannot keep your life in sight.

So stop this mess
it's horrendous
Why war? Why war
What's it for?
What does it gain?
Only pain.

Ed Ansell (12)
Hanham High School, Bristol

Green Machine

There was a boy called Sam
Who dropped a packet of ham
He didn't put it in a bin
Instead he called his friend Jim.

There was a boy in the rainforest
Whose name was Boris
He stood on a leaf
That was made out of beef
That was the end of Boris.

There was a girl called Pearl
Who liked to help the world
She helped too much
And then she ended up in a bunch.

Ben Wallace (12)
Hanham High School, Bristol

Litter

What has this world become?
Litter everywhere, it's just scum.

Litter makes the world look dirty
I don't want to look at it till I'm thirty.

Put your rubbish in the bin
If you don't, it's a sin.

If we do pick it up
In a minute we could fill a cup.

So go out and clear it up today
And when you've finished, shout hooray!

Nathan Gay (12)
Hanham High School, Bristol

Environments Behaviour

Litter is making the world like a bin
Without recycling we won't have a thing
Pollution stinks and tastes really bad
It makes all the people and animals feel sad
Bullying, racism and even war
Destroys people's homes and makes them all poor
Poverty, poverty, I hate it a lot
At the end of the day, it's just a big plot
For the poor, money hardly measures
For the rich, money is for pleasures
So please, please, clean up everything
There will be no litter, the birds will sing.

Jamie Horgan (11)
Hanham High School, Bristol

Litter

Why are you making me a mess?
Why don't you care?
Why don't you help me out?
After all, you live on and around me.

All I ask is you clean me, look after me and care
Is that too much to ask for?
Yes, yes, I could clean myself, but that's
Well a tricky job when you have no hands.

So please, please, help me out
After all, I am your world!

Lauren Henderson (12)
Hanham High School, Bristol

The Greener The Better

R euse the stuff that can be reused
E arth can't take all this pollution
C lear the streets of all the litter
Y ou can help make the world better
C ycle to work and school
L et's keep the countryside healthy
I nside every car there is CO_2
N ot in your bike, riding it is better
G reen is better, so don't drop litter.

William Arthur King (12)
Hanham High School, Bristol

Giving A Helping Hand!

Forest, ocean, jungle and land
Where animals live and breed
But pollution, litter is damaging their life
And your help is what they need.

Types of animals are slowly vanishing
So the land will become so bare
Give a hand and help the world
And show that you really care.

Samantha Bryant (11)
Hanham High School, Bristol

The Big Question!

Pretty colourful flowers or big business towers?
Mean horrible tourists or bears in the forest?
Big, fast cars or cyclists on Mars?
Small, buzzy bees or chopped down trees?
Homeless people shiver or the ducks in the river?

Daniel Short (12)
Hanham High School, Bristol

Me Chizzem

Litter is bad
Your mum is sad
We pollute the world
We need to recycle
Try to ride your bicycle.

Poverty stinks
They need some lynx
We love the rainforest
We hate racism
Me chizzem.

Animals are hairy
Being homeless is scary
War is hairy
I love my fairy
Whose name is Mary.

Climate change we need
We need to smoke less weed
We hate to kill animals
Don't grind them into gravel
Extinction is bad
They get it, they are sad
Let's save the world
Let's save the world.

Liam Robson (12)
Hanham High School, Bristol

Sam

There once was a boy named Sam
Who dropped a packet of ham
He fell over a can
Swallowed a pan
And now he is an injured man.

Callum O'Connell (13)
Hanham High School, Bristol

It's War

I can feel it coming
Coming through the air
Bullets speeding towards me
Blood is in the air

We lay and wait
For the devastation
Will it be next week
Or this very hour?

Screams are all around me
Whizzing through the air
We all cover our ears
Terror is everywhere.

Running through the streets
Dust is everywhere
Searching for cover
Where is my mother?

Fear overtakes me
Looking everywhere
I'm all alone
No one to care.

Hannah Jefferies & Ashley Keefe (13)
Hanham High School, Bristol

Nature - Haikus

A tearful tiger
And gone from the world of ours
Poaching kills creatures.

As every day dies
We see more creatures perish
Yet we do nothing.

Many men starving
Many men in joyful life
People still starving.

Luke Dunning (12)
Hanham High School, Bristol

Not The Bin!

Stop, stop
Don't throw away your small top
Give it to the charity shop.

What's that going in the bin?
Not the baked beans tin
Oh what a sin
Throw it in the recycling bin.

No, no, not the tricycle
I know a man called Michael
Who will help you to recycle.

Fred Moore (12)
Hanham High School, Bristol

Winter

Icy lakes frosted over
Footsteps crunching on the grass
My freezing fingertips blue and colder
Winter has come, it's here at last.

Snowballs flying through the air
Smacking me in the face
I'm cold and wet, but I don't care
My footsteps left without a trace.

It's falling smooth now, thick and fast
I'm loving here where I am
Love the present not the past
That's what my mum told me and my nan!

My jacket is soaked through and through
I shiver inside it, freezing
My hat and scarf and gloves too
I won't go inside, I'm *not* leaving.

Rebecca Callow (11)
Ixworth Middle School, Bury St Edmunds

Summer

Summer, summer, sizzling summer
The tap's got stuck, call the plumber
In the mood for drink
I couldn't even stop to think
Turn off the heat
The sun sizzles like my feet
On the hot summer's day
It's the perfect day to play
Heat like one million of the sun
Come on, it's time for fun!

On the warm summer's night
The wolves howl in fright
Like a tree being cut down
Pine scent through the air and I frown
There's nothing like a summer's day
To wipe all the frowns away
To think about the winter cold
To watch your curtain drapes fold
To think of the autumn leaves
To think about arrested thieves
To dream of the spring water.

Yasmin Bridges (11)
Ixworth Middle School, Bury St Edmunds

Autumn

The leaves are falling withered and dead
Falling on the ground like a ton of lead
Children running round and round
Jumping on the leaves that are on the ground
Adults shouting, 'Come in please
You're all covered with grease and leaves.'

Kieran Blakey (12)
Ixworth Middle School, Bury St Edmunds

Summertime

The sun is shining, the birds are singing
And the smell of barbecues wafts over the hedge
A neighbour starts his lawnmower
And a bird flies over the chimney pot
Someone's pruning their roses with the gentle snip,
                                snip of the secateurs
Someone opens their window to take a breath of fresh air
Ice in lemonade gently melts
Cars rumble past, their windows down, too hot to stay still
The trees offer the only shade, cooling down cyclists and walkers
Deer graze gently on the edge of a forest
Rabbits play in the wind, whilst a hawk glides gracefully over a hill
Oh how I love summertime.

Natasha McCarthy (11)
Ixworth Middle School, Bury St Edmunds

Summertime

Bright sun shines
Yellow light
Cool summer breeze
Blows away the night.

Morning brings with it the dawn
So the sun may shine till dusk
Summer's as long as an endless road
As valuable as an elephant's tusk.

The trees so green beside the lane
The garden coloured like an art
How shiny is the windowpane
How happy is my heart!

Alastair Reith (11)
Ixworth Middle School, Bury St Edmunds

Sensational Seasons

Walking in the winter
Over the crisp cold snow
Sunbathing on the beach
Swimming in the sea.

Newborn lambs on the farm
Dew sprinkled on the grass
Flowers sprouting into bloom.

All the different colours of the rainbow
Inked into the leaves
Crunchy autumn leaves
Falling off the trees.

Sensations, seasons come
Round again.

Hannah Wright (12)
Ixworth Middle School, Bury St Edmunds

Summer Days

When the sun shines high in the sky
And the heat of the day is intense
The shorts and the T-shirts and swimsuits
The warm-suited clothes all make sense.

When people are enjoying the weather
With constant trips to the beach
Children playing in the water
And eating fruit, such as mango and peach.

Summer is my favourite season
With the sun and the heat of the day
When everyone's feeling cheerful
And relaxing on beautiful bays.

Anna Reeves (10)
Ixworth Middle School, Bury St Edmunds

As Months Go By

The sun is up
The wind is bitter
It's getting hotter
And coming nearer.

It's here at last
The baking sun
I'm getting a tan
But now it's gone.

The air is getting colder
The days are getting shorter
The leaves are falling off the trees
It's almost over, here comes the breeze.

The snow has come
The footprints made
And that is it
The final days.

Emma Victoria Simpson (12)
Ixworth Middle School, Bury St Edmunds

Sensational Seasons

Summertime and the living is easy
The summer wind is warm and breezy!

Wintertime and the living is cold
Snow falling, big, white and bold.

Springtime and the living is hopping
All the flowers are growing, there's no stopping.

Autumn time and the living is a bore
The leaves are falling all over the floor.

Rachel Herod (11)
Ixworth Middle School, Bury St Edmunds

Sensational Seasons

First of all autumn
And all those lovely leaves
Yellow, brown, orange and red
And all leading up to winter.

Next we have winter
And all of that snow
We'll build snowmen
And have snowball fights.

Third, we've got spring
And my birthday month
Flowers are blooming
And leaves are on trees.

Last of all summer
Best season of the year
Sunshine and trips to the beach
What a lovely year!

Sophie Rochford (11)
Ixworth Middle School, Bury St Edmunds

My Favourite Seasons

Leaves that crunch under your feet
That cover the ground like a beautiful sheet
Sun shining, weather quite warm
Back to school, to friends in your form.

What a wonderful sight, it's a butterfly
Cute newborn lambs come skipping by
Beautiful flowers are beginning to grow
Clear blue streams flow.

Alice Neal (12)
Ixworth Middle School, Bury St Edmunds

Splendid Seasons

The autumn leaves which crunch and blow
The April showers and winter snow
The summer months which just flow like the melted snow
But now the year is through
What are we going to do?

Alexander Cattanach (12)
Ixworth Middle School, Bury St Edmunds

Seasons!

Season one is generally cold
Season two has secrets to unfold
Season three is usually hot
Season four is usually not
What are the seasons?

Emily Findlay (12) & Rosie Hopkins (11)
Ixworth Middle School, Bury St Edmunds

Spring

Warm times to enjoy
Playing on the fields, the girls and boys
Flowers blooming everywhere
Look, it's spring and the forest and a bear!

Rainy days make us sad
Time to call up Uncle Chad
What can we do to kill some time?
Paint a picture, wow, that's sublime!.

Connor Jones (12)
Ixworth Middle School, Bury St Edmunds

Summer

In the summer we have lots of fun
Digging dirt and stuff
Running around everywhere
We never have enough.

If we get wet we don't complain
If there's a drought we'll never moan
If it's stormy we'll never whinge
If it's windy we'll never groan.

Well this is the end of my poem
I hope you enjoyed it a lot
I say farewell to those who liked it
And also to those who do not.

Joshua Flack (11)
Ixworth Middle School, Bury St Edmunds

Winter Wonderland

Cold breezy day
But cosy in all different ways
Snowy blankets lay on the grass
Waiting for the season to pass
Icy cold weather
Snow as light as a feather
Put on your boots
Hear the owls hoot
Put on your hat
Wipe your feet on the mat
Dark, cold nights
What a beautiful sight!

Megan Jones (11)
Ixworth Middle School, Bury St Edmunds

Sensational Seasons

Newborn piglets on a farm
Little lambs in a barn
Proud mother sheep
Making a leap.

It's hot in the summer
Spring's gone, oh bummer
Playing tennis with a ball
Just run, don't crawl.

Leaves falling from the trees
Hitting all the bees
It's getting colder
As animals get older.

The ground is turning white
Don't fly a kite
This year has been great
I hope spring doesn't come late.

Ellie Brookes (12)
Ixworth Middle School, Bury St Edmunds

Penguins Should Be Free

Penguins should not be hurt
By that, all the icebergs might go in just one spurt
Poor, poor penguins they could fall
Global warming really drives them up the wall.

Just turn off your lights
Even at night
And all the penguins are happy
So they won't be all snappy.

Let them be free
So that they can live at the age of three.

Billy Ashford-Webb (12)
Lakeside, Chandlers Ford

The War

War is bad
War is sad
It makes us mad.

Stop it now!

People die
People cry
People fry.

Loads and loads!

Talking's better
Write a letter.

Sort it out!

Jamie Burgess (14)
Lakeside, Chandlers Ford

Noooo!

My name is Nathan, I'm here to say
Don't be racist any day
It is bad
It makes people sad
If they're adult or just a lad.

Don't be racist
Please don't do it
It gets worse
Bit by bit.

Don't be racist
Knock on their door
Say you're sorry
Or it will lead to war!

Nathan Moroncini (12)
Lakeside, Chandlers Ford

I Am A Frog

I am a frog
Peaceful and calm
Perfect home
Happy life

Cups of tea
Table of food
Evening story
Tucked in bed

Boom!

I am a frog
Petrified and frail
No more home
Ruined life

Mechanical monster
Tarnished ground
Running scared
Where to go?

I was a frog
Peaceful and calm
Vanished home
End of life.

Josh Harrison (14)
Mangotsfield School, Bristol

War

Armed soldiers running through the forest
Gunfire wailing past their heads
Far cries of scared civilians
Being murdered in their beds.

Bombshells crashing into houses
Orders sailing out of soldiers' mouths
Scattered bodies on the ground
More soldiers regrouping in the south.

Tanks patrolling forest roads
The night turns cold and black
Turrets firing left and right
Escaped civilians avoiding the track.

As dusk arrives slow and steady
Gunfire starts to arrive
More and more people getting killed
Few are still alive.

Many people have lost their lives
Many creatures too
These people just can't stop killing
Except from maybe a few.

As the war grows to a close
The light begins to fade
The soldiers start to travel home
Civilians can come out the shade.

Luke Bessell (14)
Mangotsfield School, Bristol

Terrorism

The newspaper says the enemy is amongst us
Taking our women and taking our jobs
All reasonable thought is being drowned out
By the non-stop fighting, bombing and baying for blood
I was an ordinary man with ordinary desires
I watched TV, it informed me
I was an ordinary man with ordinary desires
There must be accountability
Desperate and misinformed
Fear will keep us all in place.

Dan Upton
Mangotsfield School, Bristol

The Green Earth Dance

Here's a point you have to agree
Please don't take it personally
The human race is being a fool
By burning up the fossil fuels
Destroying the Earth's atmosphere
This is something *you* must fear.

Some people in the human race
Are bringing us to a bigger disgrace
Their clothes are designer non-stop
Made by children in a sweat-shop
Do you know what makes me most upset?
Some of them don't care about the global warming threat.

Some people in the worldwide nation
Don't stop and think about the next generation
They'll have to deal with the mess we made
All the problems we create won't just fade
So stop it whilst you have the chance
Come on, do the green Earth dance.

Katie Smart (13)
Mangotsfield School, Bristol

The Warming Of The Earth

It is here, we've been chucked in an oven
We're heating up all of a sudden

Carbon dioxide - CO_2
Blankets the Earth and melts the igloo

Polar bears having no land to stay
No fish to eat, oh what a dismay!

Hurricanes, tornadoes, floods and droughts
Worse than eating my mother's sprouts.

Cars, pollution, traffic jams
Maybe we should go back to using trams?

Save the Earth for our kids' sake
Help to stop this huge mistake!

Charlotte Wotton (13)
Mangotsfield School, Bristol

The Polar Bear

As I swam around the deep blue sea
I was as bored as can be
Not an ice cap in sight
My body was filled with fright.

I didn't know which way to turn
My body was starting to burn
All I wanted to do was eat
I felt like I didn't have any feet.

All I wanted was a fish
If only I had one wish
I would wish for a better life
Or even for a piece of ice.

So I carried on swimming in the deep blue sea
I was still as bored as can be
And still no ice cap in sight
My body is still filled with fright.

Beth Seaford (14)
Mangotsfield School, Bristol

Cold Blood

Our feet keep on moving, our backpacks are heavy
The water is bare, our progress is steady
The enemy country are ready and strong
Their trenches are dug, the killing won't take long.

Gunshots are heard, coming from the south
We leap on the floor and close our mouths
After some time, we take cover in trees
The conditions appalling, mud up to our knees.

I take out my sniper, put it to my eye
The man in my scope is about to die
The touch of cold metal, the feel of cold blood
He falls on the floor, up comes dust with a thud.

A shout from the sergeant, we go on hands and knees
We crawl to the border, we can see the Chinese
Heads poking up from the trenches, imitating meerkats
We'll shoot them all down, there's no fear of that.

The smell of smoke from barrels of guns
I cough out the waste, deep in my lungs
We're driving them back, slowly but steadily
Keep firing machine guns, the death rate grows heavily.

The enemy shout, they begin to run
Yet again I take aim and fire my gun
The sergeant shouts, the grenades are thrown
They land in the trenches, their positions are blown.

The last of the enemy has now been killed
Their bodies lay dead, in this bloodstained field
I think of my family, I think of back home
How I wish to be there, because here I'm alone.

Jack Withey (14)
Mangotsfield School, Bristol

Desert Rats

A bullet echoed in the desert sun
This war of beliefs has begun
The intensity of the moment drilled into my head
As I soon realised I will be dead
I saw the Arabs climb over the dune
Their early demise will come soon
I pulled out my gun and aimed down the sight
The glorious battle filled me with might
This is no war but an extraordinary fight!

The stench of my own sweat seeped into my nose
And drenched my desert-camouflaged clothes
I smiled as a projectile narrowly missed my head
I shot once, that Arab was dead
More bullets whizzed past my hand
I saw another stun the sand
I pulled out my gun and aimed down the sight
The glorious battle filled me with might
This is no war but an extraordinary fight!

The sand boiled in the wavering heat
The Arabs knew they had been beat
And as I eliminated their remaining men
They reminded me of killing barnyard hens
How they're innocent and harmless near impending doom
This battle ended in an explosive boom
I pulled out my gun and aimed down the sight
This glorious bloodbath filled me with might
This is no war, but a glorious fight!

Josh Martin (14)
Mangotsfield School, Bristol

We Are The Ones That Pay . . .

I could hear the slosh under my feet
I blame this on all that heat
Distant cries from far off ice
This isn't at all very nice.

The ground seems so far below
I am now becoming slow
My food now seems far too fast
I feel I may be the last.

The wind felt as hot as fire
I feel that soon I will tire
I want to taste some lovely fish
All I need is just one dish.

Snap, bang, there goes another one
It's disappearing ton by ton
I smell only emptiness in this land
Soon this will turn to sand.

Finally I taste solid ground
Why do I hear not a single sound?
Icy icicles drip away
Why are we the ones that pay?

Fleur Sherborne (14)
Mangotsfield School, Bristol

Recycle

I am recycling
Paper, plastic and tin
To help the planet I will pledge
To compost up my fruit and veg.

Also batteries and cardboard
For waste produce - it has soared
Since the years back before when
The invention of the ballpoint pen.

I cycle leisurely back to my home
And wonder how freely that I can roam
I think of the creatures that
Are locked in litter, that is a fact.

If the communities recycle the waste
Clean up the planet, we will, post-haste
Like the wheels upon my bicycle
Around go the processes that reuse and recycle.

I imagine the stench from the rubbish pile
Why, oh why is it so vile?
If all upon this world could see
How dangerous and terrible all the waste can be.

Matthew Vicker (14)
Mangotsfield School, Bristol

Soldier

War is painful
Painful is war
War is anger
Anger is war
War is revenge
Revenge is war.

I tasted death
And death tasted me
I tasted victory
The victory I want
I tasted anger
The anger in me.

I smelt fire
The fire smelt me
I smelt victory
The victory in me
I smelt cordite
The cordite we knew.

I touched the sand
The sand that touched me
I touched the trigger
The trigger that kills
I touched my wound
The wound that touched me.

I heard the Taliban
The Taliban heard me
I heard gunshots
Gunshots that kill
I heard life
The life in my heart.

I saw bodies
Bodies like me
I saw no life
The life I did have
I saw the failure
The failure I hate.

That was it
My life had now gone
I touched the war
The war that touched me
I touched death
The death that killed me . . .

Jeron Taylor (14)
Mangotsfield School, Bristol

Lost In The Arctic

Lost in the Arctic
All I can see are thin crisps of ice
But when I reach them
They fizzle away as if they were never there
A frosty figment of my imagination
I hear nothing, for I am alone.

Bobbing aimlessly in a sea of pollution
Watching the oily colours shine like a rainbow
I sense the scent of solitude all around me
As I float around like a little lost buoy
The icy water a liquid army, surrounding me
Their weapons burn my skin like wildfire.

I blame you!

Burning all your fossil fuels
Flying to foreign countries in your tin birds
Driving your metal boxes on wheels.

I see the fumes, I feel the fumes
I feel the consequence.

Emily Rose (14)
Mangotsfield School, Bristol

Global Warming, The World's A Different Place

The world's a different place for you and me today
It's changed so much, in a few short years
Well, that's what people say.

Some say it was perfect, some say it was bad
All we know is things have changed
And we shouldn't be glad.

Water levels are rising and the world is getting hot
The planet will change, it won't be the same
And it will never be forgot.

As the water's getting hotter, it rises over the land
It crashes and falls like a group of white horses
Much further than the sand.

It smashes onto buildings, wrecking everything in its path
People are injured, left homeless and lost
There's not a single laugh.

After the water is gone, destruction and death have occurred
The world isn't right, it needs to be focused
Because right now it is blurred.

But floods aren't the end, hurricanes have begun
Burma, New Orleans, people are *dead*
Something has to be done.

The world's a different place for you and me today
But we can change it and we can help
Well, that's what people say.

Abby Instone (14)
Mangotsfield School, Bristol

Homelessness

Shivering, feeling rejected and alone
I felt the cold going straight to the bone
I sat on the dirty old floor
Yes, I am homeless, worthless and poor.

Looking around the deserted street
I felt helpless and rose to my feet
I heard shoes clacking on the cobbled path
All I want is a long, hot bath.

I smelt the waft of sweet snacks from the shop
But I couldn't even afford a mop
So I will sit here as cold as ice
Yes, I am poor and paying the price.

Lying on the bare floor felt like torture and pain
I wish I could shelter from the rain
I need tangy, tasty, gingerbread men
I'm not going to get that with a penny or ten.

Shivering, feeling rejected and alone
I still feel the cold going straight to the bone
I will still sit on the old dirty floor
I will be homeless for evermore.

Izzy Walkley (13)
Mangotsfield School, Bristol

Polar Bear

Polar bears glow in the evening night
A battle against the cold, they must fight
Twinkling stars, the dazzle of the night
The whisper in the wind, what a wonderful sight.

But for polar bears, it's coming to an end
My message of worry I must send
For the ice is breaking a little each day
This is a concern I must say.

So what shall glow within the night?
When there is not a polar bear, not one in sight!

Samantha Douglas (13)
Mangotsfield School, Bristol

The Polar Bear

Water, water, water
All I can see is water
A crystal blue blanket
Covers as far as I can see.

Swimming, swimming, swimming
Is all I seem to be doing
Nothing besides thin pieces of ice
That break with a single touch.

Struggling to stay above water
The splashes of desperation
Pierce the silent sea
Becoming weaker at every stroke
Along a never-ending road.

Cold, tired and hungry
The emotions that inhibit our bodies
Wonder flows across the mind
Will this ever end?

Rebecca Brain (14)
Mangotsfield School, Bristol

Change

Forests, fires, homes being destroyed
Though this can change
Keeping trees, lowering CO_2
We can change.

Ozone melting, rubbish everywhere
Though this can change
Using public transport, recycling
We can change.

Inky-blue skies turning black
Though this can change
Using less oil, losing less lives
We can change.

Beautiful world melting away
Though this can change
Making slight changes in our lives
This is change.

Katherine Gardner (11)
Marlwood School, Bristol

How To Make The World A Better Place

E arth is decaying, dying
N ever test on animals
V ile gas is polluting our world
I rritating factories spreading across the world
R ecycle, reduce and reuse
O xygen is running low
N ow is the time to save the planet
M end our planet
E verybody needs to take part
N ever drop litter
T he world is where we live, *look after it!*

Emily Priday (11)
Marlwood School, Bristol

How To Make The World A Better Place

Global warming is swarming, the CO_2 is forming
The ice caps are melting, the polar bears are shouting
Temperatures are heightening, heat waves are firing
Stopping CO_2 will be tiring.

There is not enough fuel to guzzle
It's part of the puzzle
If we could get rid of CO_2 without a trace
That would make the world a better place.

We can't be sure if we can stop the war
But world peace, we can have at least
War can be frightening just like lightning
No war would make the world a better place.

The pollution in our ocean is like a terrible potion
All of the pollution is corrupting evolution
If we don't act now, things could go foul
If we stop dumping all over the place
It would make the world a better place.

Alex Luke (11)
Marlwood School, Bristol

How To Make The World A Better Place

E arth is struggling for breath, gasping for air
N o one realised the damage they were doing until it was too late
V anquished, by ignorance, extinguished by us
I am guilty, you are guilty, we are guilty
R oaming the land in our big jumbo-jets
O zone layer taking the blow
N etting our fish
M onkeys with no homes
E xtinction is on the rise
N o one realised the damage they were doing
T ill it was too late.

Matthew Holliday (11)
Marlwood School, Bristol

How To Make The World A Better Place

Earth is polluted
Vile gas polluting the world
Factories spreading

Animals dying
Do not test on animals
Near to extinction

Turn off all switches
Help the planet live longer
Make a difference now.

Katie Moore (11)
Marlwood School, Bristol

Compost Bins

Compost bins
Hide multiple sins

Tea from yesterday, old salad
And roses from last Valentine's Day
Didn't want them anyway
Or his attempted ballad.

Compost bins
Means everyone wins

Helping the Earth
From my old rubbish
Last week's results - already published
Hardly a celebration of anyone's mirth.

Compost bins
Are perfect
For potato skins.

Emma Johnson (17)
Newlands Girls' School, Maidenhead

Potato Skins

Travelling in a shopping bag
Of course we're not in a car
My new owner is walking home
Saving the world, what a star!

She brought me back in a recycled bag
(She doesn't believe in plastic)
I thought she was a kind owner
But then she did something drastic!

She started to peel me, I asked her to stop
But she left me yellow and bare
And I saw my lovely winter coat
Being taken out of my care.

I am going to be roasted for dinner
My word, it does sound grand
But I'm happy to know my lovely old coat
Will go back into feeding the land.

Zoë Jacobs (16)
Newlands Girls' School, Maidenhead

Eco-Fighters

E co-fighters recycle and don't use their
C ars to travel, this helps to stop burning a hole in the
O zone layer!

Hannah Cheeseman (12)
Newlands Girls' School, Maidenhead

Litter

Put litter in the bin
So animals don't get stuck in them
Don't drop litter, put it in the nearest bin
So everyone is happy
Everyone is happy
Because you are doing your bit
Environment is important
So do your bit
If you see litter, put it in the bin
Animals die because of litter
The animals get stuck
And everyone is upset
Especially if it is theirs
They also get ill if they eat out of date food
Please put litter in the bin.

Amy Stockford (12)
The Castle School, Bristol

Rainforest Trees

Tell the world to stop cutting down trees
You could make the world say please
Cutting down trees is really bad
You could make them really sad
Putting them back would be really nice
You could save all the mice
Open your eyes
And you will realise.

James Gay (12)
The Castle School, Bristol

What If . . .

What if we don't recycle?
What if it stops our life cycle?
What if the temperature gets too high?
What if we all keel over and die?
What if the sky turns black?
What if everybody gets the sack?
What if the water levels get up and about?
What if we all get flooded out?
But . . .
What if we all turn off a light?
What if our futures could still be bright?
What if we all did our bit for the town?
Let's recycle, reuse and go green for the crown!

Georgia Honey (12)
The Castle School, Bristol

Important World Matters!

Recycle bottles
Paper, food waste and plastic
Stop litter right now, please.

Chopping down trees
Robbing animals of their homes
Cruel, horrible, heartless.

Drop it on the floor
It doesn't matter, drop it
Wrong, pick it up now.

Climate change will kill
Stop CO_2 emissions
Or pay the big bill.

Stop the pollution
It's lethal, it's dangerous
Before we all drown.

Elisabeth Caise (12)
The Castle School, Bristol

What To Recycle

Clogging up your dustbin
Taking over the landfills
Plastic
Soon pollution's going to win.

Uneaten food piles high on your plate
Using up your bin space
Food waste
How long is global warming going to wait?

Recycle bottles, paper and old clothes
To keep the world going round
Recycling
When global warming strikes, no one knows!

Freya Shearman (12)
The Castle School, Bristol

2012 . . .

2012, 2012
It's the worst
The world's going to burst
Volcano, radiation, who knows?

Figure out what we're for
For once in your life
Learn more and more.

Finally, we could see
The end of the galaxy.

Recycle, recycle
It could help you and me
And our friends the trees.

Green, green
We're all so mean
So put in a bin
And keep it clean.

Brenna Harcom (12)
The Castle School, Bristol

Stop; Now Think!

Scramble, squadron scramble,
As aircraft soar machine guns chatter,
Never missing,
Mowing down all those lives with one single burst.

Shells pumped out from smoke-wreathed artillery,
Screams join the thunderous sound,
Corpses fall to the ground,
Ambulances join the frenzy.

Lives wasted away,
Screams of bombs falling from the heavens.
Raining, raining, high explosive bombs.

Trees form the opposition
Staring moodily at the scene,
Man, sawing down 100 trees a day
Shaving away the forest,
Destroying wildlife, habitats literally washed away
Must stop, full stop.

The situations
All at present
Both destroying the world we live on
Make it stop, now, think!
What can you do?

James Baxter (12)
The Castle School, Bristol

Untitled

If you want the world to be clean and green
You've got to listen to the poem machine
If you cut down our trees you will find it very hard to sneeze
If you don't litter our world will look like glitter
If you steal people's cars, you would end up behind bars.

Matthew Whiles (11)
The Castle School, Bristol

Recycle, Recycle

Recycle, recycle, recycling so cool
You can't forget that the world is so small
To save the planet, here's what you do
Recycle, recycle, recycling so cool.

Take your bottles to the bottle bank
There they can be made again
Into something else
So that's what you should do!

Recycle, recycle, recycling so cool
You can't forget that the world is so small
To save the planet, here's what you do
Recycle, recycle, recycling so cool.

Put your paper in the green bins
So you don't die with a sin
Don't throw away your old clothes
Give them to charity in lots of rows.

Charlie Tilleard & Hannah Gibbens (13)
The Castle School, Bristol

Why?

Why eat and hunt me?
Why kick and punch me?
Why have me every lunch?
Why make my bones crunch?
Why dress me up as a clown?
Why leave me stranded in a town?
Why whack us against a wall?
Why treat us like a bouncy ball?
Why abuse us like poor trees?
Why make us tremble on our knees?
Why pick on us?
Why make a fuss?
Why not let us be free?

Emily Savery (11)
The Castle School, Bristol

Our World

We hear about it on TV
Climate change and poverty
People without a place to sleep
Lie on the ground counting sheep
Or eating tea from a bin
Letting this happen is a sin.

Children dying on the streets
Are much more polite than the ones we meet
Who call each other names because of their colour
Don't care that they're hurting one another
Everyone should be treated the same
These are people's lives, not just a game.

Melting mountains because of the sun
People freezing and only just hanging on
Every day the world is polluted a lot
Like another year lined up and shot
We complain it's too hot and it's too cold
Whilst the world is dying and getting old.

We need to save the planet from its destruction
This is not advice, but an instruction
We also need to help the countries in poverty
Even though they are so far out to sea
Treat everyone the same, we are all human
These things matter, we need to start caring.

Natasha Skinner (12)
The Castle School, Bristol

Save The Rainforests

Rainforests are made of trees
Creatures, animals and wildlife
Cutting down our sources of oxygen
Is quite a big sacrifice.

Animals live there
That makes it their neighbourhood
How would you feel if it got cut down?
I would be upset, I know I would.

Make a petition
To help the forest
Go on a mission to save the world
You may be known as the boldest.

Cutting down trees is horrible
Sick, disgusting and unacceptable
Save the world, be a hero
You could end up on adverts for Aeros.

Sophie Vaughan-Williams (12)
The Castle School, Bristol

Recycle

R ecycling helps save our planet
E xtinction of animals could come soon
C lutter nutters aren't so good
Y ou can do it, so do your job
C oming together to help our planet
L itter, litter everywhere, pick it up and do your share
E co-friendly, we need to be.

Izzie Boulton (13)
The Castle School, Bristol

War Again!

Waking up and cannot bear to see
A world full of catastrophe
Round and round in your head
When you're laying in your bed
And then the sirens go again
My head is feeling pain
The big poetry machine
That's what we need
Stop this now
Don't ask how
You have just heard
Can you hear the chirping bird?
That's because you helped a lot
Even all those dirty bombs
Have gone away with the cons
Now it's only in a book
With the wicked, wicked cook.

Amy Follows (11)
The Castle School, Bristol

Our World

Our world is an amazing place
Something in every corner
So much to see and do
So, why ruin a place
Especially for me and you?

When you see Earth from space
It looks like such a lovely place
But if you look deeper, then you will see
How many problems there seem to be.

We need to do something before it gets worse
So please help our fantastic world.

Alice Rose Cottle (13)
The Castle School, Bristol

War

W orld peace, will it ever be?
A id is given to the victims
R age surges through the poor and innocent

M ake it stop please
A nger crazes people into more
K indness is the key to everything
E njoy being friends with everyone

I nnocent people brainwashed into killing
T oday, make it stop

S tarved to death, the way war destroys food and people
T oday, make it stop
O pen your heart to make it stop
P lease, please stop war . . .

Matt Roberts (12)
The Castle School, Bristol

World's Creation

The world changes every day
Children coming out to play
Sun shining on their heads
Pollution, things dying - now they're dead!

Small creatures, God's creation
Wildlife running round in the nation
Climate changing around us all
Just help the environment before it falls.

Enemies fighting at war
In the end it's such a bore
Colours of skin and changing styles
Criminal records on their files.

Hannah Coghlan (13)
The Castle School, Bristol

Rainforests

Rainforests being chopped down
The trees hit the ground
The birds fly away
Ready to come back another day
They all now have no homes
They are all starving and just skin and bones.

Stuart James (13)
The Castle School, Bristol

Save Our World

The climate is changing
The world's rearranging
The floods are getting higher
Forests are on fire
We need to recycle
But no one ever cycles
People are dying
Everyone is sighing
So please help our world
Thank you.

Ella-May Cleaver (12)
The Castle School, Bristol

The Sun Is Out

The sun is out
The sky is blue
There is not a scrap to spoil the view
But it's dying, dying in my eyes
And it's dying, dying in my hands.

Ella King (13)
The Castle School, Bristol

Animals And Extinction

A nimals and extinction
N ever to be seen again
I mmense pollution
M otion of death
A cid rain deteriorating buildings
L ush rainforests getting destroyed

A nd animals' homes getting demolished
N othing they can do, helpless
D ying in pain

E nvironment burning
X pelled from the world
T urning evil, was human now monsters
I ll-treating the world
N ever to be human again
C losed off by demons
T hat destroy every living thing they see
I hate it
O ff to war with humans but losing
N ot everyone is involved.

Sam Mindenhall (12)
The Castle School, Bristol

Save Your World!

The beaches are getting hotter
The rainforests are getting barer
The war's still on and there's lots and lots of litter
It's harming all the animals
It's too hot for dogs and the polar bears are dying
There's people on the streets starving for food
Begging on train stations of London
Do you want to grow up unsafe and unwell?
So do something about it
Because *we need your help!*

Jemma Campbell (12)
The Castle School, Bristol

Emptiness Inside Me

It's wet, it's cold
There's puddles on the ground
The moon lights up the sky
There is no human sound.

I'm shivering, I'm freezing cold
I have no more blankets
The night goes on, on it goes
Eventually the morning comes.

People are walking, around and around
I'm just sitting there alone
I shout for change, 10ps, 20ps, 1ps I ask
All I want is shelter for my home.

I dream for warmth, shelter I pray
I hope for food every day
I want a family, someone to love
But these are just dreams, I'm asking for.

Katie Walker (13)
The Castle School, Bristol

About Pollution

Green should be the colour of our world
But it is spoiled by pollution
Darker and darker every day
What are we going to do?
Pick up the litter that you drop
The mess you leave is unsatisfactory
We use too much electricity
We need more wind turbines.

We have become so lazy now
We need to walk a lot more
Not use cars, we need to keep healthy
And lastly, look after our world.

Luke Panting (12)
The Castle School, Bristol

Make It Better

Horrible litter on the floor
Pollution being made
Some are silly and ignore
We have to make a change.

Make a fresh start
Let us live properly
Be top of the charts
Don't be so naughty.

We want the smile on our face
So don't turn it upside-down
Make the world a better place
Clean up your act in town.

Cardboard and cans
We don't ask much
Recycle it up
Change our lives.

Iris McNeill (13)
The Castle School, Bristol

Rainforest

Rainforest
Once a place of beauty
Rainforest
Now a place of destruction
Rainforest
People can call it home
Rainforest
Full of exotic animals
Rainforest
It will soon be like animals, extinct
Rainforest
Act now!

Jody Wheeler
The Castle School, Bristol

How To Save The World

Paper, cans and cardboard
Making the world a better place
Recycle lots, even a sword
This is an urgent case.

Fill your green bin every week
Full of garden waste
It might make your bin reek
But not full of paper paste.

Newspaper is a good one
For a world that's safe and green
It will help the shining sun
For a world that's pure and clean.

So work today for a brighter tomorrow
One that we might never see
Think of what the world will become
Don't ruin one that was never to be.

Hannah Moore (13)
The Castle School, Bristol

Ty-Rap

If you wanna stay clean
Keep your house green
Keep your garden clean
With evergreen
Put your litter in the bin
Close the tin.

Rubbish, rubbish everywhere
Everyone's unaware
Rubbish, rubbish everywhere
And no one seems to care.

Yasmin Thatcher & Natasha Taylor (13)
The Castle School, Bristol

Recycling And Helping Saves Lives

Not being green is way too mean
Do not litter and make your life bitter
If you've got a recycling bin use it, don't abuse it
If you don't recycle you're making everyone's lives a misery
If you don't recycle, you'll feel awful and guilty
If you don't recycle, don't make it a habit
If you do recycle, you're making the world a better habitat
Although the world is still an extraordinary place
People are starving
People are dying, you must feel bad
You could change their lives forever
All you have to do is *help* in any way possible.

Christopher Hopkins (12)
The Castle School, Bristol

Save Our Planet

Pollution, climate change
Let's make sure we help
Save the planet
Make the planet a better place.

Turn off lights
Use your bikes
Help stop the planet
Being like a burning ball of pollution.

Recycle everything you can
Don't let our planet go down the pan
Bottles and glass and everything else.

Help our rainforests, keep them green
We need to keep our planet clean.

Make sure our planet stays clean and happy
Make sure you recycle that baby's nappy
Save the planet now!

Hannah Mansfield (12)
The Castle School, Bristol

The Human Contribution

Out to the country
So fresh, so green
Farmland, fields forever
Like nothing you have ever seen.

Animals everywhere
Some farm some wild
Cows and cattle to birds and bees
Place so peaceful, temperature so mild.

Into the city
It's loud, dull and grey
Busy streets full of people and cars
And is where the homeless people lay.

Litter fills the streets
Makes the smell so bad
Pollution making smoky clouds
It makes some people sad.

A lot of people do not care
What bad cities can be
To the environment and the whole world
Like killing the fish in the sea.

All the people in the world
Contribute to all of this
It brings animals to extinction
And harms the rainforests.

The huge human empire
Is an extremely large thing
We have got to try and change
Because the world can't change back in a ping.

Paige Sanders (13)
The Castle School, Bristol

Why Should Animals Suffer?

Every day animals are dying
Elephants are killed for their tusks
Tigers are killed for their skin
Whales and dolphins are trapped in unwanted nets.

Ice melting and global warming
Polar bears dying
The change of the temperature is killing
The ice is melting.

Big factories destroying the rainforest
Animals' habitats changing
Their homes being cut down for paper
Water supplies are running low
Why should animals suffer
So we can live better?

Recycle your things
Stop hunting the animals.

Victoria Hardy (12)
The Castle School, Bristol

Pollution

P ollution, pollution everywhere
O ver, under everything
L itter lying all around
L et's tidy up the world
U sing less electricity would stop it
T akes everybody to stop it
I t comes out of car exhausts
O ut and about travelling everywhere
N o one knows where it goes.

Matthew Baker (12)
The Castle School, Bristol

Tomorrow's World

Time is slipping through our fingers
like sand in an hourglass
Every second gone is lost,
we can't stand by and let it pass

Every second we must make count,
everything we do and say
We have to think whilst we still can,
we cannot carry on this way

All the modern ways of men
are not what they used to be
The planet wasn't made for this,
we carry on unnaturally

The problem is, we rush so much,
we always have to be somewhere
No one ever stops to think
or simply sit in open air

Oh no, we simply haven't the time
is what we always seem to say
We all need more than twenty-four
hours in a day.

Hannah Cornford (13)
The Castle School, Bristol

A Rare Sight

Sparkling colours in the depth
They leave behind a trail of bubbles
Floating their way to the surface of the water
Swimming through seaweed.

Creating waves above the surface
Weaving through each other
Never bumping once
A steady stream of pattern

But sadly never seen.

Cate Welmers (12)
The Castle School, Bristol

When Will They Learn?

A small planet
Seen from above for thousands of years
By only the peaceful wind gliders
Meadows, forests, oceans and seas
Left alone by all.

Take only what is needed
So nature carries on in the perfect balance
Death is followed by birth
Changing all the time
Changes seemingly invisible
But ones that made an impact . . .
Far in the future.

These brains came not fully formed
The changes of evolution reached out
More intelligent in each generation
They used themselves and each other
To change this knowledge, improving thoughts
To make progress happen.

This all seemed great at first
Then a problem would appear
Thousands spent to fix it
Only for these people to go again
And make a hole somewhere else.

When will they learn?

Sophie Romain (12)
The Castle School, Bristol

Rainforests Today And Tomorrow

Torrential rain falls upon the sodden forest floor
The humid atmosphere makes small seeds germinate
Macaws' calls echo around gnarled trees
Gasping at the hot, crisp air
Jaguars prowl through strangling ivy and vines
Clear azure rivers lick the mossy undergrowth
Animals gaze at their own reflections
Is this not natural perfection?
Trees crash, animals become extinct
Babies fall from their homes in the trees
Crashing to their death
Is this the future we want?

Sam Crow (13)
The Castle School, Bristol

Heat And Holes

Hotter and hotter
Everything changing
Icebergs melting
Temperatures ranging.

Gases spiralling
Hole in the ozone
Recycling dwindling
Traffic increasing.

Deforestation expanding
Aeroplanes discharging
Electricity booming
Climate change!

Joseph Lee (12)
The Castle School, Bristol

Rainforests

R educe rainforest fires
A lways pick up litter
I n case an animal chokes on it
N ever litter
F orever the world is changing
O n the land the litter is gaining more and more
R ubbish
E very piece of litter is destroying the world
S top littering
T o stop destroying the world we must reduce rubbish
S o think about what you are doing!

Zack Weekes (12)
The Castle School, Bristol

Cars Are Bad - Haiku

Pollution is here
We need to get rid of cars
Or we're gonna die!

Tom Child (11)
The Castle School, Bristol

War - Haiku

Death is everywhere
Explosions killing people
Faces of agony.

Shells falling
Destruction for families
People fall and die.

Wait for a second
Stop this useless fighting
Think, stop all wars.

Arran Riordan (12)
The Castle School, Bristol

Rainforests

R ainforests are like life-savers
A ll so tall and powerful
I n the world they are the heart
N ever stop growing, never stop helping
F or all this, what do they get?
O f everything they could get . . . nothing
R ainforests are homes for animals, people, insects
E veryone is affected by this horror
S creeching lives to a halt
T he green, strong, multi-tasking plants
S o stop murdering and start helping!

Jessica McLachlan (12)
The Castle School, Bristol

Extinct?

Plastic bags and rubbish, can kill fish
Get caught up, then served on a dish.

Dodos were the first to be extinct
So could other birds they think.

Let's stop it now, before it's us
Don't drive, catch a bus!

Turn off lights and go for a walk
Spread the news and talk.

Listen carefully to what I said
Then you can sleep softly in your bed.

Help, there's global warming
Be green and we could live till morning!

Meghan Young
The Castle School, Bristol

Help The Environment!

H elping the environment is
E asier than you think. As they say it's the
L ittle things that make a big difference so we can all
P ut some effort in

T ry to help make a better future for us and all mankind
H elp by recycling, don't throw away paper. For
E xample, any paper you have hardly written on put in a
  scrap paper bin

E ven the small things you put in a recycling bin can be used to make
N ew things like cans and
V arious plastic items
I magine what we could do in the next few years to slow down
  global warming if we all
R eact to all of these warnings and do something about it
O ver the next year see what you could do so save paper and energy
N ow and make our world a
M uch better place for
E veryone. If we all do our bit it will make a huge difference
  to our future but we must act
N ow before it is too late
T o do anything. *So help save the environment!*

Rachel Ling (12)
The Castle School, Bristol

Pollution Power

Pollution is *bad* for the world
Turn off your lights when you're not in the room
Instead use the light of the moon
Pollution is *bad* for the world
Go on a bus instead of your car
But if you don't, don't go far
Pollution is *bad* for the world
Put your litter in a bin
If you do, you will win
Pollution is *bad for the world!*

Jessica Nightingale (13)
The Castle School, Bristol

Global Warming

G lobal warming is such a worry
L ack of care, you need to share
O ur buses
B uses could save our houses
A ll of our houses could disappear under water
L ocal buses could save many Arctic animals

W alking to school absolutely rules
A rctic animals' lives are extremely fragile
R unning to school could be also cool
M um and Dad don't get in your Jags
I ce and icicles are stuck with Arctic animals
N othing is stopping you from reducing your carbon footprint
G o to school, walk to school, run to school
　　It is really, really cool.

Matthew Weaver (12)
The Castle School, Bristol

Rainforest

R educe forest fires
A lways pick up litter
I n case an animal chokes on it
N ever litter
F orever the world is changing . . .
O n the land, the land is gaining more and more
R ubbish
E very piece of litter is destroying the world
S top littering
T o stop destroying the world you need to recycle litter
S o think about what you are doing!

Shane Gray (12)
The Castle School, Bristol

Recyling

R ecycling is good
E veryone can do it
C an
Y ou? People do it
C ause it makes a
L ess polluted and green
E nvironment

Be green and recycle!

Jamie Lockett-Butters (12)
The Castle School, Bristol

Poverty

Over the years in Africa people die
But we still go on telling a fat lie
Every time we waste our food
They go round looking for food
That's just rude
We live and live with nothing but water
And they live on with muddy Coca-Cola.

Ana Vunipola (11)
The Castle School, Bristol

Save The Rainforests

Rainforests destroyed
Poor animals left homeless
Save the rainforests
Not enough trees alive
Too much CO_2 around.

Steven Alderton (12)
The Castle School, Bristol

War

War doesn't determine who's right, but left
When all the innocents become bereft
Small kids playing outside, still wearing diapers
Shot down by heartless men with unrelenting snipers
Leaving the helpless in a situation that's chronic
All thanks to bombs, nuclear and atomic
Soldiers wishing it will go on no more
Yet people vaguely re-enact it on 'Call Of Duty 4'.

The world can be cold, bold men take actions
You have to react or get blown into fractions
Pull the pin and throw another grenade
They get more powerful after every decade
There's bombs on the buses, bikes, roads
Inside your markets, cars and clothes
It's ironic, at times like this you pray
But a bomb blew the mosque up yesterday.

Alexander Bond (12)
The Castle School, Bristol

Get Our World Green

Let's get our world green
Let's get people keen
To save our planet
Across every nation
We need to help our next generation
So let's get together and put up a fight
Turn lights off, you're not using at night
Recycle, recycle, do not waste
Recycle, recycle, the box from the toothpaste
Global warming is coming fast
Icebergs melting, seas rising
But if we do nothing
The consequences will not be surprising.

Josh Grotzke (11)
The Castle School, Bristol

Animal Cruelty

Thousands of animals are captured every month
Helplessly unable to escape
Not understanding what's going on
Not understanding what's yet to come
Let them free, let them free.

Poked and prodded, hurt and ignored
Alone, afraid and often starved
Not cared for, not loved
Let them free, let them free.

Surely they don't deserve this?
Leave them alone, let them be
Put them back where they came from
Save them from a life of suffering
Let them free, let them free.

Just think about what you're doing next time
Think about yourself
You wouldn't like it if it was you
I'm telling you
Let them free, let them free.

Samantha Olden (14)
The Romsey School, Romsey

War

My anger, my pain
Brought on by their game
As they drop their capsules of death
I'm being forced to grow up
My innocence has left
Their pride blinds their eyes
And deafens their ears
So they can't hear our cries
What does it even mean?
This word that they use
To justify, to cover up
To compensate for
The truth behind that one syllable . . .
War!

Roya Shadmand (13)
The Romsey School, Romsey

Come On

Nature is dying nearly every day
C'mon let's help keep death away
Rainforest, pollution, it just isn't good
C'mon let's save the deep dark wood
Recycling can help in every way
C'mon stand up, it's time to say
Let's keep our world, let's keep it nice
Now it's your turn to roll the dice
Global warming is on its way
We'll soon be able to count the days.

Courtney Self (12)
The Sholing Technology College, Southampton

Their Shouts, Their Cries, Their Screams

I hear their shouts about the colour of my skin
What am I?
I hear their cries about my religion
What am I?
I hear their screams about my home-town
What am I?
Discriminated!

Francesca Saunders (12)
The Sholing Technology College, Southampton

Don't Call Me

Sticks and stones may break my bones
But words can really affect me
Don't call me black
Don't call me white

We are just the same
I can win
Not by my skin
Because personalities are stronger
Don't call me black
Don't call me white.

Because we are like the ocean
Moving as one to the solution
Don't call me black
Don't call me white
Don't call me anything than human.

Alyna Wadsworth (12)
The Sholing Technology College, Southampton

When The Aliens Came To Invade

When the aliens came to invade I was shocked
To see they haven't stayed
I searched and searched and then I found
All the pollution which is around.

When the aliens came to invade I was shocked
To see they haven't stayed
I searched and searched here and there
To find little homeless kids everywhere.

When the aliens came to invade
I'll tell you why they haven't stayed
It's how we treat the world so bad
Which is what made them really mad.

Sorcha Hoey (12)
The Sholing Technology College, Southampton

Recycling

New things come and go
But not all people recycle, so
You use the nature of the world
By filing it up with litter.

Animals lose their homes
When humans chop their habitats down
To fill more and more junk
Soon the world will overload.

So please recycle your rubbish
Even one piece of litter recycled
Could save the world!

Charlotte Collinson (12)
The Sholing Technology College, Southampton

Animals Live!

Habitats everywhere
Crowded in forests
Not enough for them all
How do they survive?

Monkeys swing on trees
Tigers hunt
Pandas climb trees
Giraffes eat leaves.

Elephants' horns
Bears growl
Lions roar
It's wildlife here!

Emma Clement (12)
The Sholing Technology College, Southampton

Nothing There

I'm on the streets
Nothing there
I'm on my own
Nothing there
I beg for money
But nothing is there
All I want is something there
But still it ends up with nothing there
Where's my family?
But nothing there . . .
And still nothing there.

Isabelle Taylor (11)
The Sholing Technology College, Southampton

Do The Right Thing

Please do not drop litter
It makes the world bitter
People always die of hunger
Why, I wonder?
You! Don't throw that in the bin
Put in the recycle bin
And please stop cutting down the trees
The world needs them to breathe
Trees are homes for lots of animals
And koalas too
And in the autumn, the leaves turn golden for me and you
Some people are so unhealthy
But some others are wealthy
Why is the world so unfair?
Maybe more people should care.

Stephanie Dale (12)
Wentworth College, Bournemouth

Racism

In the world there are black and white
But don't forget the brown
If we live in harmony
There will be peace around.

The Arabs travel in the desert
Avoiding the heat of the day
At the same time
Eskimos slowly skate away.

The world would be a better place
If we respected others
I'm going to make a better world
By treating each other like brothers.

Sophie Poll (12)
Wentworth College, Bournemouth

The Green Machine Rap

We are the big green poetry machine
We like to keep the whole world looking clean
We pick up litter so streets gleam
Poverty is the worst thing the world's ever seen
Racism is ever so mean!

Turn off the lights, it'll save you money
The state of the world, isn't very funny
Give food to the homeless, it will fill their tummies
Don't smoke or pollute, it will harm pregnant mummies
Don't test drugs on animals like bunnies!

We need a solution to all this pollution
So fill them green bins, recycle those tins
Change the world today
And forever it will stay!

Natalie Bray & Georgina Anthony (15)
Wildern School, Southampton

Last One Down

He runs, he jumps, he travels
In leaps and bounds and strides
He hears the bad man coming
Then scurries off and hides.
His friends are disappearing
And now it's no surprise
He hears the bad man coming
And looks into his eyes
He's gone like all the others
A head above a fire.

Jack Randall (15)
Wildern School, Southampton

A Homeless Cinderella

'Move along, move along, you can't stay here
Come on, you can spend the night elsewhere.'
They keep moving me onwards, never upwards
I'm always going to be here
Under a blanket
On my own
My only company from the passers-by, who always stop and stare
They look at me, half in rage and half in fear
All I wanted was a family to love me, a home I could call my own
My bed, a cardboard box, so tender and so dear
I just hope it doesn't rain
It always rains, even though the skies are clear
Always with the wrong crowd, they lie and cheat and steal
I wish that I could just go home, to those who love and feel
But they could never love me, for I was their Cinderella
Who has now found her homeless prince.

Charlotte Dilworth (14)
Wildern School, Southampton

The Station

An Afro-Caribbean taking a pew
But doesn't realise he is about to be stew
A gang of youths come up to him
About to commit a deadly sin
A train is heading down the line
As a youth pulls out a shiny nine
Sitting there with a gun in his face
Only because he is a different race
The trigger gets pulled and he falls to the floor
The youths run away to be seen no more
His body lies there on the platform
Another family's pride has now been torn.

What was the point in this discrimination
That was shown that day down at the station?

Christopher Ball (14)
Wildern School, Southampton

Save The World

Cars are making greenhouse gases
Rubbish is being dumped in masses

Deforestation is a complication
So try and help the nation

Living in a tree
Is not too easy

There are worldwide disasters
They can't be fixed with plasters

Recycle paper
It can make a difference later

So save our world we live here now
To help the environment you know how!

Sacha Speed (14)
Wildern School, Southampton

Possibilities

Houses falling from the cliffs
Climate change
People worry the world will end
The world will not end
At least I don't think so.

Trees give us life, so help them live
Save us, don't use as many trees
Use the used paper for the recycle bins
If you don't recycle waste, it will go to waste.

Fill the bins with your tins
Recycle your cans and they will make a car
And so the possibilities are endless
If you don't waste, the UK won't stink
So help the world last longer.

Tom Watts (12)
Wildern School, Southampton

Racism

At school hidden in the corner it happens
I can see kicking, punching
Tears welling up in his eyes
He doesn't cry, he can't
Or the bullies will kick harder.

Colour and race need not be a barrier
Towards friendship and fun
Be friendly, we are all the same
Even if it doesn't show
Their image is who they are
It makes them special.

Nina Cable (13)
Wildern School, Southampton

Child Abuse

Don't hide from it, face the facts
There is no need for child abuse
Kids commit suicide
Stop it now
No education
No food or drink
Poor shelter and homes
Children are made as slaves
Children will pass it on if they are abused
Children hurt and even crying
Make the world a better place today.

Dan Fountain (12)
Wildern School, Southampton

The Polluted Earth

Fiery, fierce pollution flowing through the Earth
Gases diffusing in the misty air
Families wishing it could stop
But powerful people have no care.

The ozone layer is getting thinner and thinner
Climate change, cold, warm and hot
Emerging in the cities
Damaged cities suffer and die.

Extinction of animals rising
Oil leaking, dripping in the sea
Smelly, disgusting pollution
Pollution, pollution, pollution.

Dangerous lethal fuels burning, releasing
One day the world will rot
But nobody cares
Pollution, pollution, pollution.

Iphigénie Compton (12)
Wildern School, Southampton

Poverty

Starvation
Infection
Diseases
Shanty towns
Sadness hangs over people in need
Death is round every corner
Shivering with no clothes on
Unimaginable conditions
Sadness hangs over people in need.

Lewis Gray (13)
Wildern School, Southampton

The Lies Of War

Joining in the fight, so that our country may live another day
The dark lies that lay beneath our feet
Death upon death clouding the sky
Explosion upon explosion lighting the sky with death
Bodies surrounding us in the midnight rain
The bitter taste of taking lives, surrounding the luxury of still having ours
The empty shells lie dead like the soul you lost
Pain is all you can feel
The light fades in the shadow of our shame
We have no choice but to kill, for it is the only way to survive
Gunshots are the only thing heard apart from pain or suffering
The life of pride lost in fight
Training prepared us for the flight, but not the loss of life
The light blazes as we say our final words
Surrounded by the enemy, our mission is at an end . . .

Nathan Matterson (13)
Wildern School, Southampton

The Homeless

They have no food to eat
Just the dirty remains left in a bin
People scrounge to get enough money to survive
They sit all alone
There is no life in their eyes
Just sitting remembering what they once had
The bitter wind bites at their skin
The cold takes effect
There is no shelter to turn to
They are weak and can barely stand
They beg all day long
Wearing old ragged clothes
They cannot afford anything better!

Emily Banks (13)
Wildern School, Southampton

What Is Wrong With The World?

Seems a normal day, the worst is still to come
Soldiers recruited right out of school
I must be brave for those I love.

Parents scared, almost to death
It makes us crazy, it ruins our brain
Why must it be like this?

Scared and confused, why is this happening?
Just want to go home to my parents' arms
Crying and crying about what will happen.

Weaker and weaker, my heart is pounding
Guns and violence taking over
It will make you or break you.

Impossible to get out, have to fight
War will take our lives
Get out while you can.

Dexter Eden (13)
Wildern School, Southampton

Drug Users

Homeless, dirty, scary
Hidden down sallow alleyways
Alone with only a needle for comfort
They smile, they seem happy
But their eyes tell the lies.

Lauren Exall (12)
Wildern School, Southampton

War Is All Around Us

War is all around us
Mothers cry
As their children die
War is all around us.

War is all around us
Young men in camps training to kill
This shouldn't be the path they chose
One of wrong and ill
War is all around us.

War is all around us
Men are traumatised
Watching friends fall and die
War is all around us.

War is all around us
Men come back different
Not harder, weaker
War is all around us.

War is all around us
The scars are not just skin deep
There is more to it than that
War is all around us.

Many men come and go
But the ideas stays the same
To find a better way to kill
Again and again and again.

Ben Heer (13)
Wildern School, Southampton

Just Come Home And Stay Home

Wives and children mourn the deaths
Dressed in black for the day they say goodbye
So many men hoped to come home alive
So many graves, so many tears.

There's so much more to do in life
So why the constant arguing?
By the end, your life may just end
Never wind up in this situation.

Guns reloading, repeating clicks
Bullets fly through the sky
Ground destroyed by exploding bombs
Men fall to the floor and don't get back up.

Peace is like glue between paper
Some now have the chance to go home
You don't need to stand on the bloody battlefield
Just imagine the world without it all.

Megan Brown (13)
Wildern School, Southampton

Drugs

When they come for you
It will be life in prison
You'll be unwanted
Inflicting on others
Drugs cost money
Down alleyways and on street corners
They find you shivering with an overdose
Unclean needles and infections
One dose can kill you
Sniff and your life is gone!

Isabelle Short (12)
Wildern School, Southampton

Nothing

We walk along the streets and see
Homeless with nothing to do
Begging for money
Scavenging for food
Cold in the night
People feeling sorry for you
Others laugh as they pass
Your friends?
You have none
Your family?
Can't you find them?
How come it came to this?
Shivering under a cloth, a thin cloth
No one to turn to
Nothing to call your own
How do you survive?

Alice Chant (13)
Wildern School, Southampton

Bullies

Hurting, punching, kicking,
Excuses, excuses.
This is what a bully is!
Excuses, excuses,
Blackmailing, stealing, lying.
Excuses, excuses.
A bully is a coward!

Aimée Virgo (13)
Wildern School, Southampton

The Arctic Ice Giant

Huge magnificent giants walking along the ice
Baby fluffy polar bears following their mums
Their superbly magnificent size
Protecting their young.

You can keep it.

Too tame with humans will result in death
New age threats such as pollution
Global warming equals habitat loss
One lonely bear looking lost.

You can stop it.

Their pain growing with every gunshot
The fear in their deep brown eyes
A deafening roar
Starving to death.

You can help it.

Decreasing numbers
You can change it!

Megan Buckle (13)
Wildern School, Southampton

Lives Will Be Lost

Can you stop war and save lives?
If you can do it now, maybe you'll save your own life
Stop seeing children dead after war
Stop the homicides, killings and waste of lives
Making the world more peaceful again
If you don't stop it now, lives will be lost!

Frazer Vella (13)
Wildern School, Southampton

What Has Happened?

Hungry people starving to death
As skinny as a stick with their ribs showing
Scavenging on their hands and knees
Screaming for help!

Crouched over in a cold damp corner
Others chattering to one another
Knocking and banging on wooden doors
Shelters shattering and falling to the ground.

Buildings and homes crumbling to the ground
Sniffing as the wind blows onto their faces
Food scattered around all over the place
Surrounded by destruction!

Screeching and yelling, crying and moaning
Homeless and fighting for their lives!

Jess Angel (13)
Wildern School, Southampton

Homeless

No friends, no money, no family
Crouching up in corners
Meeting strangers all the time
Living in cardboard boxes
Begging for any spare change
The darkness of night is near
Sat alone in the freezing cold wind
Watching everyone go past
Laughing with all their friends
Who have you got?
No one
Praying in the cold rain
Asking for everything that you can get
Smelling as something is rotting
Worrying about what is to come . . .

Charlotte Bowen (13)
Wildern School, Southampton

Home Away From Home

Alone, all alone
Being scared, unwanted and sad
Not knowing what lies ahead.

Sleeping on the hard, cold floor in the empty street
Shivering and shaking in the dead of night
Feeling so lonely and uncomfortable.

No one there to help you in your time of need
Wind blowing and whistling into the darkness of the night
The bitter cold biting at your fingers and feet.

Waiting, listening to the scratching and rustling
Of the creatures lurching in the bushes
Finding shelter from the bitter cold and harsh winds
Hard to battle for life, not death.

Would you switch places?

Rebecca Williams (13)
Wildern School, Southampton

Looks

People may be different
Black or white
But you shouldn't make fun of them
Because we are all the same inside.

It shouldn't matter
What you look like
You shouldn't abuse
You should protect.

If you see someone being abused
Stand up, speak up
Think about how people feel
Because of their race.

We all live together
In the same society.

Tremayne Moore (13)
Wildern School, Southampton

A Child's Nightmare

Nowhere to go when the rain pours down
People live with harsh weather conditions
A baby cries in the middle of the night
Is there anyone to look after him?

Vulnerable babies having nothing to eat
Nothing to protect them from the world outside
Homeless people crowd the street
Will anyone give them what they need?

We can't walk away from this hopeless situation
So, look up and listen, it won't go away
Will you help give them what they need?
Will you help charities look after them?

Children die before they reach their teens
But we all deserve to live our lives
We need to help everyone in our world
Help the children that are in poverty.

Alarna Harris (13)
Wildern School, Southampton

Global Warming, Global Warning

We may be different from our skin to our race
But we are all the same belonging to the human race!

So stop the ice caps melting, whether north or south
They belong to all of us, so help!

Even though we're far away, the rainforest still exists
The flowers help with medicine, so don't destroy it all!

The Earth's becoming hotter, far too hot for some
With unexpected weather just around the corner!

A way to help is to recycle, just change the bin you put it in
So be a friend of the Earth!

Clover Pelling (13)
Wildern School, Southampton

Think War

Here at war I don't know what to think
Should I think about the unbearable heat
Melting our every chance?
Should I think about the innocence lost
As civilians get caught in the crossfire?
Should I think about their funeral
As we remember that fatal shot with every tear?
Should I think about my fellow soldiers
Who I trust with my life?
Should I think about feeling guilty
Wondering if I am doing the right thing?
Should I think about that everlasting fear
Wondering if the next moment could be your last?
Should I think about tomorrow
As every new day shows a glimmer of hope?
Should I think about the Union Jack
Its bold colours powering us through the pain?
Should I think about being proud
Fighting for Queen and country
Or should I think about the thought
The thought of never seeing you again?

Yes, this is war
No game, no joke
I just want to go home.

Jessica Parlour (13)
Wildern School, Southampton

Lives Of War

The silver moon beams down and protects the soldier
Bombshells fall from the sky
The black powerful guns lined up in a row
Glimmer in the sun's blinding light
The sharp, short sound of guns going off
The deafening moaning of soldiers injured and ill
Murdered by the Queen's word
The vulgar taste of death
Not enough sleep
Haven't got anything to eat
Lonely and cold
Belief and hope
Image of home and people alone
The smell of victory or not
I want to go home.

Carly Mason (13)
Wildern School, Southampton

Poverty

Poverty is bad
It is the anger inside waiting to strike.

Poverty is everywhere
In the city and even in the house next door.

Poverty is in the city
Where people lay and die on the doorsteps outside.

Poverty can happen to us all, even you or I.

James Foot (13)
Wildern School, Southampton

Extinction

She will be extinct
She will
She will

Fish dying in the sea
Pollution

He will be extinct
He will
He will

Whales being hunted for food and blubber
Whaling

They will be extinct
They will
They will

The crocodile and cheetah being shot for their skins
Poaching

We will be extinct
We will
We will
We will.

Sully Hill (13)
Wildern School, Southampton

Young Writers Information

We hope you have enjoyed reading this book - and that you will continue to enjoy it in the coming years.

If you like reading and writing poetry drop us a line, or give us a call, and we'll send you a free information pack.

Alternatively if you would like to order further copies of this book or any of our other titles, then please give us a call or log onto our website at www.youngwriters.co.uk

**Young Writers Information
Remus House
Coltsfoot Drive
Peterborough
PE2 9JX**

(01733) 890066